Mometrix
TEST PREPARATION

I0868205

MCA

Success Strategies
Grade 8
Mathematics

DEAR FUTURE EXAM SUCCESS STORY

First of all, **THANK YOU** for purchasing Mometrix study materials!

Second, congratulations! You are one of the few determined test-takers who are committed to doing whatever it takes to excel on your exam. **You have come to the right place.** We developed these study materials with one goal in mind: to deliver you the information you need in a format that's concise and easy to use.

In addition to optimizing your guide for the content of the test, we've outlined our recommended steps for breaking down the preparation process into small, attainable goals so you can make sure you stay on track.

We've also analyzed the entire test-taking process, identifying the most common pitfalls and showing how you can overcome them and be ready for any curveball the test throws you.

Standardized testing is one of the biggest obstacles on your road to success, which only increases the importance of doing well in the high-pressure, high-stakes environment of test day. Your results on this test could have a significant impact on your future, and this guide provides the information and practical advice to help you achieve your full potential on test day.

Your success is our success

We would love to hear from you! If you would like to share the story of your exam success or if you have any questions or comments in regard to our products, please contact us at **800-673-8175** or **support@mometrix.com**.

Thanks again for your business and we wish you continued success!

Sincerely,
The Mometrix Test Preparation Team

Written and edited by the Mometrix Test Preparation Team
Printed in the United States of America

TABLE OF CONTENTS

Introduction

Thank you for purchasing this resource! You have made the choice to prepare yourself for a test that could have a huge impact on your future, and this guide is designed to help you be fully ready for test day. Obviously, it's important to have a solid understanding of the test material, but you also need to be prepared for the unique environment and stressors of the test, so that you can perform to the best of your abilities.

For this purpose, the first section that appears in this guide is the **Success Strategies**. We've devoted countless hours to meticulously researching what works and what doesn't, and we've boiled down our findings to the most impactful steps you can take to improve your performance on the test. We start at the beginning with study planning and move through the preparation process, all the way to the testing strategies that will help you get the most out of what you know when you're finally sitting in front of the test.

We recommend that you start preparing for your test as far in advance as possible. However, if you've bought this guide as a last-minute study resource and only have a few days before your test, we recommend that you skip over the first two Success Strategies since they address a long-term study plan.

If you struggle with **test anxiety**, we strongly encourage you to check out our recommendations for how you can overcome it. Test anxiety is a formidable foe, but it can be beaten, and we want to make sure you have the tools you need to defeat it.

Strategy #1 – Plan Big, Study Small

There's a lot riding on your performance. If you want to ace this test, you're going to need to keep your skills sharp and the material fresh in your mind. You need a plan that lets you review everything you need to know while still fitting in your schedule. We'll break this strategy down into three categories.

Information Organization

Start with the information you already have: the official test outline. From this, you can make a complete list of all the concepts you need to cover before the test. Organize these concepts into groups that can be studied together, and create a list of any related vocabulary you need to learn so you can brush up on any difficult terms. You'll want to keep this vocabulary list handy once you actually start studying since you may need to add to it along the way.

Time Management

Once you have your set of study concepts, decide how to spread them out over the time you have left before the test. Break your study plan into small, clear goals so you have a manageable task for each day and know exactly what you're doing. Then just focus on one small step at a time. When you manage your time this way, you don't need to spend hours at a time studying. Studying a small block of content for a short period each day helps you retain information better and avoid stressing over how much you have left to do. You can relax knowing that you have a plan to cover everything in time. In order for this strategy to be effective though, you have to start studying early and stick to your schedule. Avoid the exhaustion and futility that comes from last-minute cramming!

Study Environment

The environment you study in has a big impact on your learning. Studying in a coffee shop, while probably more enjoyable, is not likely to be as fruitful as studying in a quiet room. It's important to keep distractions to a minimum. You're only planning to study for a short block of time, so make the most of it. Don't pause to check your phone or get up to find a snack. It's also important to **avoid multitasking**. Research has consistently shown that multitasking will make your studying dramatically less effective. Your study area should also be comfortable and well-lit so you don't have the distraction of straining your eyes or sitting on an uncomfortable chair.

The time of day you study is also important. You want to be rested and alert. Don't wait until just before bedtime. Study when you'll be most likely to comprehend and remember. Even better, if you know what time of day your test will be, set that time aside for study. That way your brain will be used to working on that subject at that specific time and you'll have a better chance of recalling information.

Finally, it can be helpful to team up with others who are studying for the same test. Your actual studying should be done in as isolated an environment as possible, but the work of organizing the information and setting up the study plan can be divided up. In between study sessions, you can discuss with your teammates the concepts that you're all studying and quiz each other on the details. Just be sure that your teammates are as serious about the test as you are. If you find that your study time is being replaced with social time, you might need to find a new team.

Strategy #2 – Make Your Studying Count

You're devoting a lot of time and effort to preparing for this test, so you want to be absolutely certain it will pay off. This means doing more than just reading the content and hoping you can remember it on test day. It's important to make every minute of study count. There are two main areas you can focus on to make your studying count.

Retention

It doesn't matter how much time you study if you can't remember the material. You need to make sure you are retaining the concepts. To check your retention of the information you're learning, try recalling it at later times with minimal prompting. Try carrying around flashcards and glance at one or two from time to time or ask a friend who's also studying for the test to quiz you.

To enhance your retention, look for ways to put the information into practice so that you can apply it rather than simply recalling it. If you're using the information in practical ways, it will be much easier to remember. Similarly, it helps to solidify a concept in your mind if you're not only reading it to yourself but also explaining it to someone else. Ask a friend to let you teach them about a concept you're a little shaky on (or speak aloud to an imaginary audience if necessary). As you try to summarize, define, give examples, and answer your friend's questions, you'll understand the concepts better and they will stay with you longer. Finally, step back for a big picture view and ask yourself how each piece of information fits with the whole subject. When you link the different concepts together and see them working together as a whole, it's easier to remember the individual components.

Finally, practice showing your work on any multi-step problems, even if you're just studying. Writing out each step you take to solve a problem will help solidify the process in your mind, and you'll be more likely to remember it during the test.

Modality

Modality simply refers to the means or method by which you study. Choosing a study modality that fits your own individual learning style is crucial. No two people learn best in exactly the same way, so it's important to know your strengths and use them to your advantage.

For example, if you learn best by visualization, focus on visualizing a concept in your mind and draw an image or a diagram. Try color-coding your notes, illustrating them, or creating symbols that will trigger your mind to recall a learned concept. If you learn best by hearing or discussing information, find a study partner who learns the same way or read aloud to yourself. Think about how to put the information in your own words. Imagine that you are giving a lecture on the topic and record yourself so you can listen to it later.

For any learning style, flashcards can be helpful. Organize the information so you can take advantage of spare moments to review. Underline key words or phrases. Use different colors for different categories. Mnemonic devices (such as creating a short list in which every item starts with the same letter) can also help with retention. Find what works best for you and use it to store the information in your mind most effectively and easily.

Strategy #3 – Practice the Right Way

Your success on test day depends not only on how many hours you put into preparing, but also on whether you prepared the right way. It's good to check along the way to see if your studying is paying off. One of the most effective ways to do this is by taking practice tests to evaluate your progress. Practice tests are useful because they show exactly where you need to improve. Every time you take a practice test, pay special attention to these three groups of questions:

- The questions you got wrong
- The questions you had to guess on, even if you guessed right
- The questions you found difficult or slow to work through

This will show you exactly what your weak areas are, and where you need to devote more study time. Ask yourself why each of these questions gave you trouble. Was it because you didn't understand the material? Was it because you didn't remember the vocabulary? Do you need more repetitions on this type of question to build speed and confidence? Dig into those questions and figure out how you can strengthen your weak areas as you go back to review the material.

Additionally, many practice tests have a section explaining the answer choices. It can be tempting to read the explanation and think that you now have a good understanding of the concept. However, an explanation likely only covers part of the question's broader context. Even if the explanation makes perfect sense, **go back and investigate** every concept related to the question until you're positive you have a thorough understanding.

As you go along, keep in mind that the practice test is just that: practice. Memorizing these questions and answers will not be very helpful on the actual test because it is unlikely to have any of the same exact questions. If you only know the right answers to the sample questions, you won't be prepared for the real thing. **Study the concepts** until you understand them fully, and then you'll be able to answer any question that shows up on the test.

It's important to wait on the practice tests until you're ready. If you take a test on your first day of study, you may be overwhelmed by the amount of material covered and how much you need to learn. Work up to it gradually.

On test day, you'll need to be prepared for answering questions, managing your time, and using the test-taking strategies you've learned. It's a lot to balance, like a mental marathon that will have a big impact on your future. Like training for a marathon, you'll need to start slowly and work your way up. When test day arrives, you'll be ready.

Start with the strategies you've read in the first two Success Strategies—plan your course and study in the way that works best for you. If you have time, consider using multiple study resources to get different approaches to the same concepts. It can be helpful to see difficult concepts from more than one angle. Then find a good source for practice tests. Many times, the test website will suggest potential study resources or provide sample tests.

Practice Test Strategy

If you're able to find at least three practice tests, we recommend this strategy:

Untimed and Open-Book Practice

Take the first test with no time constraints and with your notes and study guide handy. Take your time and focus on applying the strategies you've learned.

Timed and Open-Book Practice

Take the second practice test open-book as well, but set a timer and practice pacing yourself to finish in time.

Timed and Closed-Book Practice

Take any other practice tests as if it were test day. Set a timer and put away your study materials. Sit at a table or desk in a quiet room, imagine yourself at the testing center, and answer questions as quickly and accurately as possible.

Keep repeating timed and closed-book tests on a regular basis until you run out of practice tests or it's time for the actual test. Your mind will be ready for the schedule and stress of test day, and you'll be able to focus on recalling the material you've learned.

Strategy #4 – Pace Yourself

Once you're fully prepared for the material on the test, your biggest challenge on test day will be managing your time. Just knowing that the clock is ticking can make you panic even if you have plenty of time left. Work on pacing yourself so you can build confidence against the time constraints of the exam. Pacing is a difficult skill to master, especially in a high-pressure environment, so **practice is vital**.

Set time expectations for your pace based on how much time is available. For example, if a section has 60 questions and the time limit is 30 minutes, you know you have to average 30 seconds or less per question in order to answer them all. Although 30 seconds is the hard limit, set 25 seconds per question as your goal, so you reserve extra time to spend on harder questions. When you budget extra time for the harder questions, you no longer have any reason to stress when those questions take longer to answer.

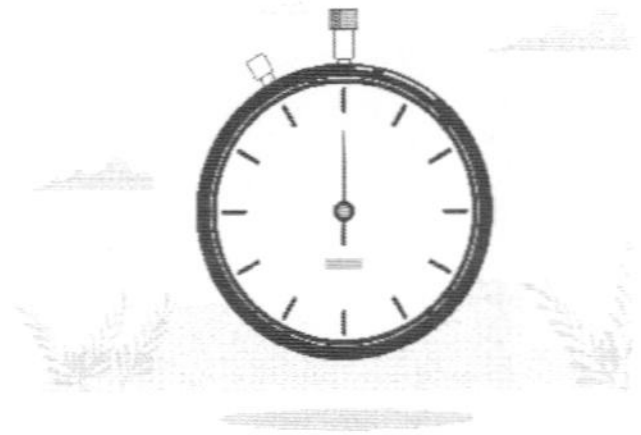

Don't let this time expectation distract you from working through the test at a calm, steady pace, but keep it in mind so you don't spend too much time on any one question. Recognize that taking extra time on one question you don't understand may keep you from answering two that you do understand later in the test. If your time limit for a question is up and you're still not sure of the answer, mark it and move on, and come back to it later if the time and the test format allow. If the testing format doesn't allow you to return to earlier questions, just make an educated guess; then put it out of your mind and move on.

On the easier questions, be careful not to rush. It may seem wise to hurry through them so you have more time for the challenging ones, but it's not worth missing one if you know the concept and just didn't take the time to read the question fully. Work efficiently but make sure you understand the question and have looked at all of the answer choices, since more than one may seem right at first.

Even if you're paying attention to the time, you may find yourself a little behind at some point. You should speed up to get back on track, but do so wisely. Don't panic; just take a few seconds less on each question until you're caught up. Don't guess without thinking, but do look through the answer choices and eliminate any you know are wrong. If you can get down to two choices, it is often worthwhile to guess from those. Once you've chosen an answer, move on and don't dwell on any that you skipped or had to hurry through. If a question was taking too long, chances are it was one of the harder ones, so you weren't as likely to get it right anyway.

On the other hand, if you find yourself getting ahead of schedule, it may be beneficial to slow down a little. The more quickly you work, the more likely you are to make a careless mistake that will affect your score. You've budgeted time for each question, so don't be afraid to spend that time. Practice an efficient but careful pace to get the most out of the time you have.

Test-Taking Strategies

This section contains a list of test-taking strategies that you may find helpful as you work through the test. By taking what you know and applying logical thought, you can maximize your chances of answering any question correctly!

It is very important to realize that every question is different and every person is different: no single strategy will work on every question, and no single strategy will work for every person. That's why we've included all of them here, so you can try them out and determine which ones work best for different types of questions and which ones work best for you.

Question Strategies

✓ Read Carefully

Read the question and the answer choices carefully. Don't miss the question because you misread the terms. You have plenty of time to read each question thoroughly and make sure you understand what is being asked. Yet a happy medium must be attained, so don't waste too much time. You must read carefully and efficiently.

✓ Contextual Clues

Look for contextual clues. If the question includes a word you are not familiar with, look at the immediate context for some indication of what the word might mean. Contextual clues can often give you all the information you need to decipher the meaning of an unfamiliar word. Even if you can't determine the meaning, you may be able to narrow down the possibilities enough to make a solid guess at the answer to the question.

✓ Prefixes

If you're having trouble with a word in the question or answer choices, try dissecting it. Take advantage of every clue that the word might include. Prefixes can be a huge help. Usually, they allow you to determine a basic meaning. *Pre-* means before, *post-* means after, *pro-* is positive, *de-* is negative. From prefixes, you can get an idea of the general meaning of the word and try to put it into context.

✓ Hedge Words

Watch out for critical hedge words, such as *likely, may, can, often, almost, mostly, usually, generally, rarely,* and *sometimes.* Question writers insert these hedge phrases to cover every possibility. Often an answer choice will be wrong simply because it leaves no room for exception. Be on guard for answer choices that have definitive words such as *exactly* and *always.*

✓ Switchback Words

Stay alert for *switchbacks*. These are the words and phrases frequently used to alert you to shifts in thought. The most common switchback words are *but, although,* and *however.* Others include *nevertheless, on the other hand, even though, while, in spite of, despite,* and *regardless of.* Switchback words are important to catch because they can change the direction of the question or an answer choice.

⊘ Face Value

When in doubt, use common sense. Accept the situation in the problem at face value. Don't read too much into it. These problems will not require you to make wild assumptions. If you have to go beyond creativity and warp time or space in order to have an answer choice fit the question, then you should move on and consider the other answer choices. These are normal problems rooted in reality. The applicable relationship or explanation may not be readily apparent, but it is there for you to figure out. Use your common sense to interpret anything that isn't clear.

Answer Choice Strategies

⊘ Answer Selection

The most thorough way to pick an answer choice is to identify and eliminate wrong answers until only one is left, then confirm it is the correct answer. Sometimes an answer choice may immediately seem right, but be careful. The test writers will usually put more than one reasonable answer choice on each question, so take a second to read all of them and make sure that the other choices are not equally obvious. As long as you have time left, it is better to read every answer choice than to pick the first one that looks right without checking the others.

⊘ Answer Choice Families

An answer choice family consists of two (in rare cases, three) answer choices that are very similar in construction and cannot all be true at the same time. If you see two answer choices that are direct opposites or parallels, one of them is usually the correct answer. For instance, if one answer choice says that quantity *x* increases and another either says that quantity *x* decreases (opposite) or says that quantity *y* increases (parallel), then those answer choices would fall into the same family. An answer choice that doesn't match the construction of the answer choice family is more likely to be incorrect. Most questions will not have answer choice families, but when they do appear, you should be prepared to recognize them.

⊘ Eliminate Answers

Eliminate answer choices as soon as you realize they are wrong, but make sure you consider all possibilities. If you are eliminating answer choices and realize that the last one you are left with is also wrong, don't panic. Start over and consider each choice again. There may be something you missed the first time that you will realize on the second pass.

⊘ Avoid Fact Traps

Don't be distracted by an answer choice that is factually true but doesn't answer the question. You are looking for the choice that answers the question. Stay focused on what the question is asking for so you don't accidentally pick an answer that is true but incorrect. Always go back to the question and make sure the answer choice you've selected actually answers the question and is not merely a true statement.

⊘ Extreme Statements

In general, you should avoid answers that put forth extreme actions as standard practice or proclaim controversial ideas as established fact. An answer choice that states the "process should be used in certain situations, if…" is much more likely to be correct than one that states the "process should be discontinued completely." The first is a calm rational statement and doesn't even make a definitive, uncompromising stance, using a hedge word *if* to provide wiggle room, whereas the second choice is far more extreme.

⊘ BENCHMARK

As you read through the answer choices and you come across one that seems to answer the question well, mentally select that answer choice. This is not your final answer, but it's the one that will help you evaluate the other answer choices. The one that you selected is your benchmark or standard for judging each of the other answer choices. Every other answer choice must be compared to your benchmark. That choice is correct until proven otherwise by another answer choice beating it. If you find a better answer, then that one becomes your new benchmark. Once you've decided that no other choice answers the question as well as your benchmark, you have your final answer.

⊘ PREDICT THE ANSWER

Before you even start looking at the answer choices, it is often best to try to predict the answer. When you come up with the answer on your own, it is easier to avoid distractions and traps because you will know exactly what to look for. The right answer choice is unlikely to be word-for-word what you came up with, but it should be a close match. Even if you are confident that you have the right answer, you should still take the time to read each option before moving on.

General Strategies

⊘ TOUGH QUESTIONS

If you are stumped on a problem or it appears too hard or too difficult, don't waste time. Move on! Remember though, if you can quickly check for obviously incorrect answer choices, your chances of guessing correctly are greatly improved. Before you completely give up, at least try to knock out a couple of possible answers. Eliminate what you can and then guess at the remaining answer choices before moving on.

⊘ CHECK YOUR WORK

Since you will probably not know every term listed and the answer to every question, it is important that you get credit for the ones that you do know. Don't miss any questions through careless mistakes. If at all possible, try to take a second to look back over your answer selection and make sure you've selected the correct answer choice and haven't made a costly careless mistake (such as marking an answer choice that you didn't mean to mark). This quick double check should more than pay for itself in caught mistakes for the time it costs.

⊘ PACE YOURSELF

It's easy to be overwhelmed when you're looking at a page full of questions; your mind is confused and full of random thoughts, and the clock is ticking down faster than you would like. Calm down and maintain the pace that you have set for yourself. Especially as you get down to the last few minutes of the test, don't let the small numbers on the clock make you panic. As long as you are on track by monitoring your pace, you are guaranteed to have time for each question.

⊘ DON'T RUSH

It is very easy to make errors when you are in a hurry. Maintaining a fast pace in answering questions is pointless if it makes you miss questions that you would have gotten right otherwise. Test writers like to include distracting information and wrong answers that seem right. Taking a little extra time to avoid careless mistakes can make all the difference in your test score. Find a pace that allows you to be confident in the answers that you select.

⊘ Keep Moving

Panicking will not help you pass the test, so do your best to stay calm and keep moving. Taking deep breaths and going through the answer elimination steps you practiced can help to break through a stress barrier and keep your pace.

Final Notes

The combination of a solid foundation of content knowledge and the confidence that comes from practicing your plan for applying that knowledge is the key to maximizing your performance on test day. As your foundation of content knowledge is built up and strengthened, you'll find that the strategies included in this chapter become more and more effective in helping you quickly sift through the distractions and traps of the test to isolate the correct answer.

Now that you're preparing to move forward into the test content chapters of this book, be sure to keep your goal in mind. As you read, think about how you will be able to apply this information on the test. If you've already seen sample questions for the test and you have an idea of the question format and style, try to come up with questions of your own that you can answer based on what you're reading. This will give you valuable practice applying your knowledge in the same ways you can expect to on test day.

Good luck and good studying!

Mathematics

Converting a Decimal with a Repeating Pattern into a Rational Number

To convert a decimal with a repeating pattern into a rational number, write the equation x = decimal number. Then multiply each side of the equation by 10n, where n is the number of repeating digits. Subtract the first equation from the second equation, and solve the resulting equation for x.

Example:

$$\begin{aligned} \mathrm{x} &= 0.207207207\ldots \\ 1000\mathrm{x} &= 207.207207207\ldots \\ 999\mathrm{x} &= 207 \\ \mathrm{x} &= \frac{207}{999} = \frac{23}{111} \end{aligned}$$

Show How to Determine the Approximate Location of an Irrational Number √N on the Number Line, Where 0 < N < 100, Without a Calculator. Include an Example.

To find the approximate location of $\sqrt{\mathrm{n}}$ on the number line, find consecutive integers a and b such that a2 < n < b2. This means that a < $\sqrt{\mathrm{n}}$ < b and the irrational number lies between a and b on the number line. If n is closer to a2 than it is to b2, place $\sqrt{\mathrm{n}}$ a little closer to a than b.

Example:

$$\begin{aligned} &\sqrt{51} \\ 7^2 &= 49, 8^2 = 64 \\ \sqrt{49} &< \sqrt{51} < \sqrt{64} \\ 7 &< \sqrt{51} < 8 \end{aligned}$$

Place $\sqrt{51}$ closer to 7 than 8, because 49 is closer to 51 than 64:

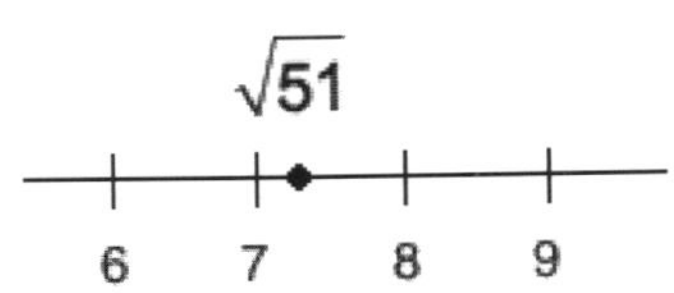

Writing the properties of integer exponents for simplifying expressions of the form $a^m a^n$, $\frac{a^m}{a^n}$, and $(a^m)^n$

The properties of integer exponents for simplifying expressions of the form $a^m a^n$, $\frac{a^m}{a^n}$, and $(a^m)^n$ are as follows:

$$\begin{aligned} a^m a^n &= a^{m+n} \\ \frac{a^m}{a^n} &= a^{m-n} \\ (a^m)^n &= a^{mn} \end{aligned}$$

The only restriction on the value of a is that $a \neq 0$ for $\frac{a^m}{a^n}$.

Perfect Square and Perfect Cube

The term perfect square means a number that is equal to the square of an integer. This means that the square root of the perfect square is itself an integer. For example, 16 is a perfect square because $4^2 = 16$, and $\sqrt{16} = 4$. A perfect cube is a number that is a cube of an integer. The number 8 is a perfect cube, because $2^3 = 8$, and correspondingly $\sqrt[3]{8} = 2$. If a number is not a perfect square, then the square root of the number is irrational. Similarly, a number that is not a perfect cube has a cube root that is irrational.

Scientific Notation

A number is written in scientific notation when it has the form $a \times 10^n$, where $1 \leq a < 10$ and n is an integer. A very small number such as 0.0000000032 can be written in scientific notation by counting the number of places the decimal point must move to the right before the value of the number is at least 1. In this example, moving the decimal point 9 places gives the value 3.2. If a = 3.2, then the exponent n must be −9 to make up for multiplying by 10^9:

$$0.0000000032 = 3.2 \times 10^{-9}$$

Notation 1E8

The notation 1E8 displayed on a calculator is in scientific notation. This is a shorthand notation that the calculator uses, so that it can fit very large and very small numbers on the screen. The letter E stands for exponent, and the number that follows the E is the value of the exponent on the number 10. The number before the E is multiplied by the power of 10 indicated. The expression 1E8 has the value 1×10^8, or 100,000,000. Note that because the number is in scientific notation, the number before the E is always at least 1 and less than 10.

Proportion

A proportion is an equation that has a ratio on each side of the equal sign. The ratios may be in the form of a fraction, such as $\frac{x}{100}$, or written with a colon, such as 3:5. For example, suppose two classes have 3 girls for every 2 boys. The ratio of girls to boys is 3:2.

To find the number of boys in a class with 25 students, write a proportion:

$$\frac{\text{number of boys}}{\text{number of students}} = \frac{2}{5} = \frac{x}{25}$$

In this proportion, the ratios represent the number of boys: number of students.

Determining the Slope-Intercept Form of an Equation for a Non-Vertical Line

The slope-intercept form of a line is $y = mx + b$, where m is the slope of the line and b is the y-intercept. The slope of the line can be determined using the formula $m = \frac{y_1 - y_0}{x_1 - x_0}$, where (x_0, y_0) and (x_1, y_1) are two distinct points on the graph of the line. To find the value of b if not known from the graph, solve the equation $y_1 = mx_1 + b$ after substituting the values for m, x_1, and y_1. Finally, write the slope-intercept form of the line $y = mx + b$ with the values of m and b substituted into the equation.

Solving a Linear Equation in One Variable

When solving a linear equation in one variable, if the process results in a true equation of the form $a = a$ where a is a real number, the equation has infinitely many solutions. This is because the equation is always true, independent of the value of the variable. For example, consider the solution of the equation below:

$$\begin{aligned} 2x - 3(x + 1) &= 2 - (x + 5) \\ 2x - 3x - 3 &= 2 - x - 5 \\ -x - 3 &= -x - 3 \\ -3 &= -3 \end{aligned}$$

For any value of x, each side of the equation evaluates to 3. So the solution is x = any real number, and there are infinitely many solutions.

Coefficient and Like Terms

It is often necessary to add or subtract terms when solving a linear equation. Like terms are terms that have the same variable part. For example, $4x$ and $-2x$ are like terms, or x terms. Similarly, $\frac{3}{4}$ and $0.2x$ are like terms. The coefficients of these terms are the real numbers that multiply the variable part. To collect like terms, add the coefficients and keep the same variable part.

$$4x + (-2x) = (4 - 2)x = 2x$$
$$\frac{3x}{4} + 0.2x = \frac{3x}{4} + \frac{x}{5} = \frac{19x}{20}$$

Different Possibilities That Can Occur Graphically for a Given System of Two Linear Equations in Two Variables

There are 3 possibilities that can occur graphically for a given system of two linear equations in two variables:

1. The graphs intersect. The point at which they intersect is the solution of the system of equations.
2. The graphs are the same, or coincide with each other. This means that the two equations are actually the same equation. The solution of the system is all points on the line.
3. The graphs do not intersect, and the system has no solution. This occurs when the two equations have the same slope, or the two lines are distinct vertical lines. These lines are parallel.

Substitution Method for Solving a Linear System of Equations in Two Variables

The substitution method for solving a linear system of equations in two variables involves solving one equation for a particular variable. Then, the expression for that variable is substituted into the other equation, resulting in a one-variable equation that can be solved. To determine the value of the other variable, substitute the value of the solved variable into one of the original equations. Example:

$x - 2y = -3$

$2x + y = -1$ Solve the second equation for y: $y = -2x - 1$

Substitute into the 1st equation:

$$\begin{aligned} x - 2(-2x - 1) &= -3 \\ 5x + 2 &= -3 \\ x &= -1 \end{aligned}$$

Substitute into the first equation:

$$\begin{aligned} (-1) - 2y &= -3 \\ -2y &= -2 \\ y &= 1 \end{aligned}$$

The solution of the system is (–1, 1).

Determining the Values of *A* and *B*, When the Sum and the Difference of Two Numbers *A* and *B* are Both 15, with *A* > *B*

The values of a and b can be determined by setting up and solving a system of linear equations in two variables. Suppose the sum of the variables is 15, and the difference is 15. Then a plus b equals 15, and a minus b equals 15. Note that $b - a$ will not work, because $a > b$, and this difference would result in a negative number. Write the system as follows:

$a + b = 15$

$a - b = 15$

Since $a > b$, write the difference as $a - b$.

Solve the system to find that $a = 15$ and $b = 0$.

Functions and Relations

Functions and relations are alike in that both are sets of ordered pairs wherein each pair is an input (the first value) and an associated output (the second value). Functions and relations are different in that a function has only one output (a "unique" output) for each input, but a relation may have more than one output for each input (the output is not necessarily unique). Consequently, functions are relations, but relations are not necessarily functions. The following sets are examples of a relation that is not a function, and a function:

- relation (not a function): {(1, 4), (2, 3), (3, 4), (1, 2)}
- function: {(1, 4), (2, 3), (3, 4), (4, 0)}

The input 1 has two different outputs (4 and 2) in the relation, so it is not a function.

Determining the Rate of Change for a Linear Function Using a Table of Values for the Function

The rate of change can be determined for a linear function using a table of values by calculating the change in the dependent variable divided by the change in the independent variable for two data points. The points can be any two points from the table. This value is also equal to the slope of the graph of the linear function. Care should be taken to calculate the change in each variable in the same direction, so that an error in the sign of the rate of change is not made. For example, if two data points from the table are (3, 6) and (5, 1), then the rate of change is 6 – 1 = 5 divided by 3 – 5 = –2, or –2.5.

Recognizing a Linear Function from Its Graph

A linear function can be recognized from its graph by noting that all of the points of the graph fall on a straight line. This means that a line drawn with a straightedge through any two points of the graph will coincide with the entire graph of the function. One exception, however, is a vertical line. Although it is straight, it is not a linear function because it is not a function. A function has a unique output value for each input value, but a vertical line has every real number as an output value for one input value.

For a linear function that models the cost to rent a canoe for a certain number of hours, the rate of change indicates the cost per hour to rent the canoe. This is because the rate of change is the change in the dependent variable, or the cost, divided by the change in the independent variable, or the number of hours. The initial value of the function gives the cost to rent the canoe for the least allowed number of hours. For example, the point (0, 0) might represent the initial value or cost of $0 for renting the canoe for 0 hours. However, if a minimum 2-hour rental was required, the initial value would be 2 times the rate of change, and the point would have an x-coordinate of 2.

Determing When the Function Is Increasing, Decreasing, and Has a Minimum Value for the Function $Y = X^2$

The graph of the function $y = x^2$ is a parabola. It takes on a minimum value of 0 at $x = 0$, which is the vertex of the parabola at (0, 0). For all negative values of x, the function is decreasing. This is because the graph falls from left to right. The graph starts to flatten out as x approaches 0. Then for all positive values of x, the function is increasing. This is because the graph rises from left to right. The further away from $x = 0$ the x-value of the function is, the greater the rate at which the function decreases or increases at that point of the function. This is evident from the steepness of the graph.

Effect of Reflecting a Vertical Line Segment in the Third Quadrant over the Y-Axis

When a vertical segment in the third quadrant is reflected over the y-axis, the reflected image is in the fourth quadrant. The image will be the same distance from the y-axis. Specifically, the x-coordinates of the image will be the opposites of the x-coordinates of the original segment, and the y-coordinates will be the same as the original segment. The length of the segment will be the same as the original segment. This is because reflections in the coordinate plane result in images that are congruent to the original figure.

An Equilateral Triangle Is Rotated Clockwise 90° About the Origin, Determe How This Will Affect the Measures of the Angles of the Triangle

A rotation clockwise of 90° about the origin will not affect the measures of the angles of the triangle. This is because for any rotation in the coordinate plane, angles are taken to angles of the same measure. In fact, the image triangle will also be an equilateral triangle, with 60° angle measures, that is congruent to the original triangle. The only angles that change are the angles related to the position of the triangle relative to the origin. Specifically, the segments from the origin to the vertices of the original triangle have rotated 90° clockwise, with the endpoint at the origin remaining fixed.

Translation of a Line in the Coordinate Plane Results in a Line Parallel to the Original Line

Suppose two points on the original line are (a, b) and (c, d). This means the slope of the line is $\frac{d-b}{c-a}$, or for $a = c$ the line is a vertical line. Translate the line m units vertically and n units horizontally. The points (a, b) and (c, d) are now at $(a + m, b + n)$ and $(c + m, d + n)$. The slope of this line is

$\frac{d+n-b-n}{c+m-a-m} = \frac{d-b}{c-a}$, which is the same as the original line, or a vertical line for $a = c$. This means the line is parallel to the original line.

Transformations can be used to prove two figures in the coordinate plane are congruent

Two figures in the coordinate plane can be proven congruent by showing there is a sequence of transformations that obtains one figure from the other. The transformations can include rotations, reflections, or translations. For each point on the original figure, the sequence of transformations takes that point to the corresponding point of the second figure. For example, if triangle *ABC* is congruent to triangle *FGH*, then the sequence of transformations takes vertex *A* to vertex *F*, vertex *B* to vertex *G*, and vertex *C* to vertex *H*. It also takes each point on every side of triangle *ABC* to each point on every side of triangle *FGH*.

A square in the coordinate plane is dilated by a factor of 2. How this will affect the coordinates of the vertices of the square and the area of the square?

If a square in the coordinate plane is dilated by a factor of 2, the coordinates of the vertices of the square will all be multiplied by 2. For example, if (3, 0) was a vertex point of the square, the dilation takes this point to (6, 0). The area of the square will be multiplied by a factor of 4. This can be illustrated by considering a square with vertices at $(0, 0)$, $(0, a)$, (a, a), and $(a, 0)$. These points become $(0, 0)$, $(0, 2a)$, $(2a, 2a)$, and $(2a, 0)$. The area is now $(2a)(2a) = 4a^2$, which is 4 times the area of the original square.

Similar figures

Similar figures are figures that have the same shape, but not necessarily the same size. If two figures on the coordinate plane are similar, then there is a series of transformations that can obtain one of the figures from the other. If the figures are not the same size, then one of the transformations is necessarily a dilation. If a dilation is not needed, then the two figures are not only similar, but they are also congruent. Similar figures such as polygons have corresponding side lengths that are in proportion, and corresponding angles that are congruent.

Pairs of congruent angles that are formed when two parallel lines are cut by a transversal

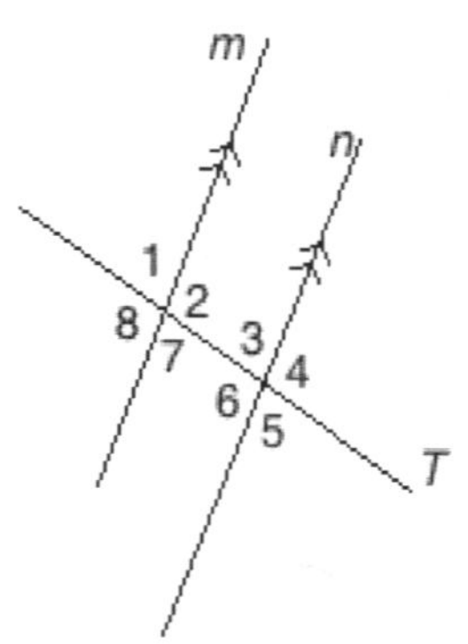

The diagram shows parallel lines *m* and *n* cut by transversal *T*. Angles 1 and 3 are corresponding angles. Other pairs of corresponding angles are 2 and 4, 5 and 7, and 6 and 8. Angles 2 and 6 are alternate interior angles, as are angles 3 and 7. Angles 1 and 5 are alternate exterior angles, as are angles 4 and 8. Angles 1 and 7, 2 and 8, 3 and 5, and 4 and 6 are all pairs of vertical angles. Each of these pairs of angles consists of two congruent angles.

Converse of the Pythagorean Theorem

The converse of the Pythagorean Theorem states that if the sum of the squares of the lengths of any two sides of a triangle are equal to the square of the length of the remaining side, then the triangle is a right triangle. The converse is applied when all three side lengths of a triangle are known, but the angle measures are not. The Pythagorean Theorem is applied when it is known that one angle of the triangle is a right angle, i.e., that the triangle is a right triangle. Then if two side lengths are known, the theorem can be applied to determine the missing side length.

Write two equations that could help solve for x and y in the diagram. What theorem is needed?

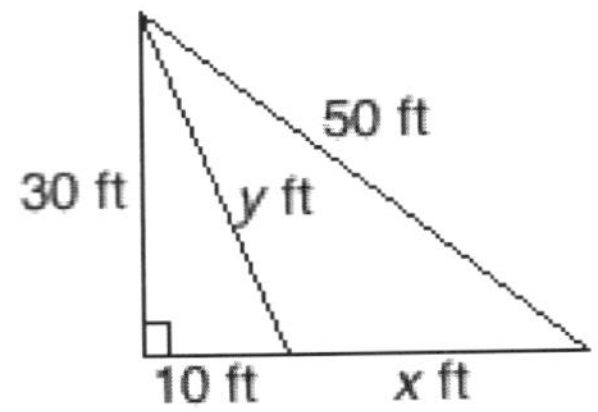

There are two right triangles in the diagram. Because x and y represent unknown lengths in the diagram, the Pythagorean Theorem can be used to solve for x and y. In the small right triangle, y is length of the hypotenuse. This gives the equation $30^2 + 10^2 = y^2$, or $y^2 = 1000$, so $y = 10\sqrt{10}$. In the large right triangle, the two segments labeled 10 ft and x ft form a leg, so the expression $(10 + x)$ represents the length of the leg. This leads to the equation $30^2 + (10 + x)^2 = 50^2$, or $(10 + x)^2 = 1600$. Since $40^2 = 1600$, $10 + x = 40$ and $x = 30$.

Apply the Pythagorean Theorem to find the distance from the origin to the point (a, b).

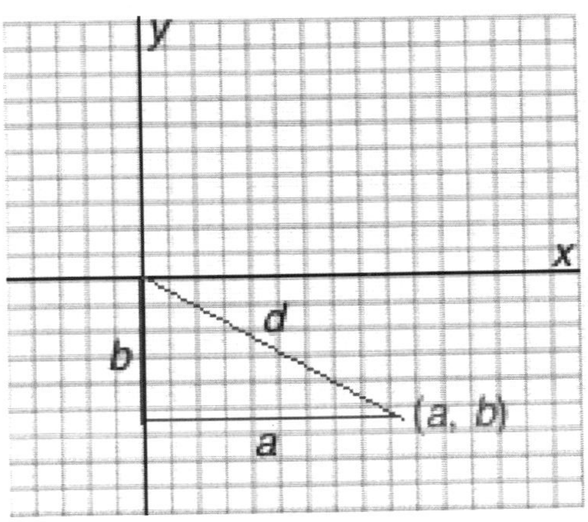

The sketch shows the point (a, b) in the fourth quadrant. Regardless of which quadrant the point is located, a right triangle can be drawn as shown. The lengths of the legs of the triangle are a and b, since the point (a, b) is a units from the y-axis and b units from the x-axis. Note that if the point (a, b) is on the x-axis or y-axis, then the distance from the origin is simply given by the value of the intercept. By the Pythagorean Theorem, $a^2 + b^2 = d^2$, and the distance is given by $d = \sqrt{a^2 + b^2}$.

Determining the weight of a bowling ball with a 4-inch radius and the material used to make the ball has a density of 0.05 lb/in³

The weight of a bowling ball can be calculated if the volume of the ball is known. The ball is in the shape of a sphere, and the formula for the volume of a sphere is $V = \frac{4}{3}\pi r^3$, where r is the radius of the ball. If the calculated volume is multiplied by the density of the material used, then the units of cubic inches will cancel. The resulting value is the weight of the bowling ball.

$$V = \frac{4}{3}\pi r^3 = \frac{4}{3}\pi 4^3 = \frac{256}{3}\pi$$

$$\text{weight} = \frac{256}{3}\pi \cdot 0.05 = \frac{64}{15}\pi, \text{ or about } 13.4 \text{ lb}$$

Univariate and Bivariate Data

Univariate data consist of one data type, whereas bivariate data consist of two data types. For example, a set of data that consists of the lengths of several fish caught in a lake is univariate data. However, if that same data also include the time of day that each fish was caught, then the data are bivariate. A scatter plot shows the graph of bivariate data, with one data type on the horizontal axis and the other data type on the vertical axis. This way, the graph can be examined to see if there is any connection (or correlation) between the two data types (or in this example, between the length of the fish and the time when the fish was caught).

Sketching a Best-Fit Line for a Scatter Plot with Data That Show a Linear Association

For a scatter plot with data that show a linear association, a best-fit line is a straight line that comes as close to all the data points as possible. To sketch the best-fit line, use a straightedge and draw a line through the points, trying to minimize the vertical distances of the points from the line. In general, about half of the data points should fall above the line, and half below the line. There may be points that fall directly on the line. If there are outliers in the scatter plot—points that do not seem to fit the data because they are very far from most of the data points—do not consider these points when sketching the line of best-fit.

A Scatterplot Shows Hours Studied for a Test on the *X*-Axis, and Test Scores on the *Y*-Axis. Interpret the Slope and *Y*-Intercept of a Best-Fit Line for the Data.

Each point (x, y) represents the number of hours studied x and the corresponding score y on the test. The slope of the best-fit line is the change in y divided by the change in x, so this is the rate of change of the score per hour studied. For example, if the slope were 10, then there is an increase of 10 points per hour studied. The y-intercept is the score when $x = 0$, i.e., when the number of hours studied is zero. If the y-intercept were 35, for example, then the best-fit line predicts a score of 35 points for a student that does not study at all.

Distinguish Frequencies from Relative Frequencies

A frequency is the number of times that an event occurs, or a data value falls into a certain category. When a frequency is given as a proportion or percentage of a population, this is a relative frequency. This means that relative frequencies give a better idea of how many data values fall into a certain group, *relative* to the population being studied. For example, suppose 50 students are asked to choose their favorite subject out of math, science, and history. The frequencies may be math = 14, science = 21, and history = 15. The relative frequencies would then be math = $\frac{14}{50}$ or 0.28, science = $\frac{21}{50}$ or 0.42, and history = $\frac{15}{50}$ or 0.30.

Rational Number

A rational number is any number that can be expressed as a ratio of two integers $\frac{a}{b}$, where $b \neq 0$. The value of b is nonzero because division by zero is undefined. All integers are rational numbers because any integer a can be written as $\frac{a}{1}$. In addition, all decimal numbers that terminate or repeat a pattern are rational numbers, because they can be written as a ratio of two integers. The numbers -4.2, $3\frac{1}{5}$, 218, and 0 are all rational numbers. Non-examples of a rational number include π and $\sqrt{2}$, both of which cannot be written as a ratio of two integers. These numbers are called irrational numbers.

Using truncation to find a rational number written as a fraction that is within 0.001 of $\sqrt{5} = 2.360679774$ .....

Truncation refers to the removal of significant digits from the right-most decimal place of a number, typically to get an approximation.

Truncating the given value of $\sqrt{5}$ after 3 decimal places gives us 2.360. This number is accurate within 0.001 because no matter what the 4th decimal place is, it represents a value that is less than 0.001. Written as a fraction, $2.360 = 2\frac{360}{1000} = 2\frac{9}{25}$.

Why the expressions $\left(\frac{1}{2}\right)^{-2}$ and 2^2 are equivalent

To show that the expressions are equivalent, simplify each expression by using the properties of exponents. Negative exponents such as -2 can be rewritten as $(2)(-1)$, and the exponent -1 corresponds to taking the reciprocal of the expression.

$$\left(\frac{1}{2}\right)^{-2} = \left[\left(\frac{1}{2}\right)^{2}\right]^{-1}$$

Use the property $a^{mn} = (a^m)^n$ to rewrite the expression.

$= \left[\frac{1}{4}\right]^{-1}$ Simplify the power.

$= 4$ The reciprocal of $\frac{1}{4}$ is 4.

The expression $2^2 = 4$, so both expressions simplify to 4 and therefore the expressions are equivalent.

Using Radical Notation to Write the Solutions to $x^3 = 16$ and $x^3 = 27$

Each equation has x raised to the power of 3. To undo this, take the cube root of each side of the equation:

$$x^3 = 16 \qquad x^3 = 27$$

$$x = \sqrt[3]{16} \qquad x = \sqrt[3]{27}$$

The numbers 16 and 27 go beneath the radical symbol. These numbers are referred to as radicands. The small 3 outside the radical symbol represents cube root. This number is called the index. The solution to the equation $x^3 = 27$ is an integer, but the solution to $x^3 = 16$ is not. $\sqrt[3]{27} = 3$ because $3^3 = 3 \cdot 3 \cdot 3 = 27$. $\sqrt[3]{16}$ is not an integer. Its value is between the integers 2 and 3, because $2^3 = 8$ and $3^3 = 27$. Using a calculator, $\sqrt[3]{16}$ is approximately 2.52.

The US gross debt increased from about 5.1×10^8 dollars in 1940 to about 1.4×10^9 dollars in 2010. Estimate how many times larger the debt in 2010 is compared to the debt in 1940.

To estimate how many times larger the debt is in 2010, write the ratio of debt in 2010 to the debt in 1940. Break up the powers of 10 and use the properties of integer exponents to simplify $\frac{10^9}{10^8}$ to 10. Multiply to get $\frac{14}{5.1}$, which is equivalent to $\frac{140}{51}$. Since 51 is very close to 50, $\frac{140}{51}$ is about $\frac{140}{50} = \frac{14}{5}$ or 2.8.

$$\frac{1.4 \times 10^9}{5.1 \times 10^8} = \frac{1.4}{5.1} \cdot \frac{10^9}{10^8} = \frac{1.4}{5.1} \cdot 10 = \frac{14}{5.1} \approx \frac{14}{5} = 2.8$$

Check the estimate with a calculator: $\frac{1.4 \times 10^9}{5.1 \times 10^8} \approx 2.745098 \ldots$

Adding Large Numbers Written in Scientific Notation

When adding very large numbers in scientific notation, special attention must be paid to the powers of 10. If the exponents on the powers of 10 are the same, then the numbers being multiplied by the powers of 10 can be added. The sum is then multiplied by the same power of 10, and then the product is rewritten (if necessary) in scientific notation.

If the exponents on the powers of 10 are different, then the smaller numbers should be rewritten to match the greatest power of 10. This is shown in the example below:

$3.854 \times 10^{29} + 8.066 \times 10^{28} =$

$3.854 \times 10^{29} + 0.8066 \times 10^{29} =$ Rewrite with the power 10^{29}.

4.6606×10^{29} Add the numbers and keep the power 10^{29}.

Henry drives 310 miles in 5 hours and 10 minutes. He says his distance-time graph shows a proportional relationship. What does this say about Henry's driving rate?

The proportional relationship is of the form $d = rt$, where r is a non-zero constant. This means the graph is a straight line through the origin with a slope of r. Henry is therefore driving at a constant rate equal to the slope r of the line graph. To determine the rate in miles per hour, convert 5 hours and 10 minutes to hours. There are 60 minutes in 1 hour, so 10 minutes is $\frac{1}{6}$ hour. The rate is given by the following ratio:

$$\frac{310}{5\frac{1}{6}} = 310 \cdot \frac{6}{31} = 60$$

Henry is driving at a constant rate of 60 miles per hour.

Use Similar Triangles to Confirm That the Slope of a Non-Vertical Straight Line Is the Same for Any Two Distinct Points on the Line

Draw a non-vertical line m on the coordinate plane. Then draw 3 distinct horizontal lines intersecting line m in 3 distinct points. Finally, draw 2 vertical lines through the two intersection points just found with the greatest y-values. The graph below illustrates this.

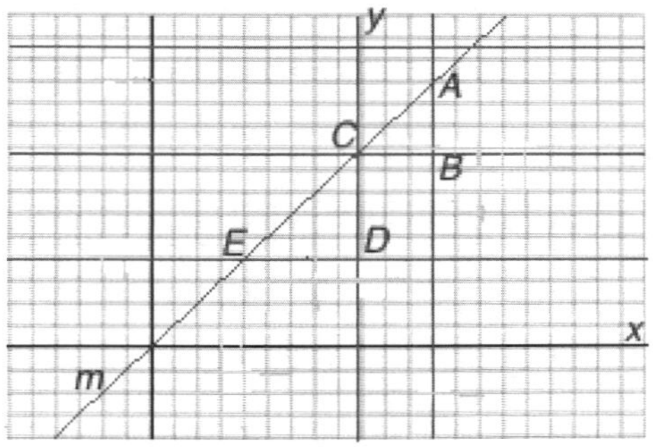

Triangles ABC and CDE are similar by the angle-angle criterion. Angles B and D are right angles, and angle ACB and angle CED corresponding angles of two parallel line cut by transversal m. Since the triangles are similar, the ratio of CD to DE is equal to the ratio of AB to BC. These ratios are the slope of line m, which means any two points will give the same slope.

When Solving a Linear Equation in One Variable, There Is No Solution

When solving a linear equation in one variable, if the process results in a false equation of the form $a = b$ where a and b are different (not equal) numbers, the equation has no solution. This is because the equation is always false, independent of the value of the variable. For example, consider the solution of the equation below:

$$\begin{aligned} 2x - 3(x + 1) &= 2 - (x + 4) \\ 2x - 3x - 3 &= 2 - x - 4 \\ -x - 3 &= -x - 2 \\ -3 &= -2 \end{aligned}$$

For any value of x, each side of the equation evaluates to two different values. The equation therefore has no solution.

Distributive Property

The distributive property is used to multiply expressions, with at least one being a parenthetical expression that has sums or differences. Algebraically, the distributive property is written as follows:

$a(b + c) = ab + ac$

$(b + c)a = ba + ca$

The distributive property is often used when solving a linear one-variable equation. This is because rewriting the products without the parentheses make it is easier to combine like terms. This is illustrated in the example below:

$2(x - 3) = 3x - 2(x + 1)$

$2x - 6 = 3x - 2x - 2$ Apply distributive property in two places.

$2x - 6 = x - 2$

$x = 4$

Ron Graphs a System of Two Equations, but the Graphs Are the Same Line.

If Ron did not make a mistake, then the equations are equivalent. He should algebraically check that he can simplify one of the equations to get the other equation. If he cannot, then he may have made a mistake graphing one of the equations. If the equations are indeed equivalent, then the graph of the system is simply the graph of the line. This also means that the solution of the system is all the points on the line, and there are infinitely many solutions. Note that this is different than the solution "all real numbers"—the solution must include the equation of the line. If the line were, for example, $y = 2x + 1$, then the solution can be written $\{(x, y) \mid y = 2x + 1\}$.

Solve the System $y = x - 1$ and $y = 1 - x$ by Inspection

The system $y = x - 1$ and $y = 1 - x$ can be solved by inspection, which means it can be solved by briefly studying the system and performing some mental math. The expressions $x - 1$ and $1 - x$ are opposites. In general, $a - b$ is the opposite of $b - a$, since $-(a - b) = -a + b = b - a$. This means that y is equal to some number and its opposite. The only number that is equal to its own opposite is zero, so this means $y = 0$. Substituting $y = 0$ into either equation gives $x = 1$. The solution of the system is $(x, y) = (1, 0)$.

How a System Can Be Used to Determine How 50 Coins Can Have a Value of \$8, if All the Coins Are Quarters and Dimes

Let q = the number of quarters, and d = the number of dimes. This means that $q + d = 50$, because there are 50 coins altogether. To write another equation so that there is a two-variable system that can be solved, use the value of each coin. Each dime will contribute 10 cents to the \$5, and each quarter will contribute 25 cents. Since \$5 is equal to 500 cents, this leads to the equation $10d + 25q = 500$. Solving this system gives $d = 30$ and $q = 20$. Note that both variables must be non-negative integers; otherwise there is no solution in the context of the problem.

The Graph of a Relation Includes the Points (3, 4) and (8, 4). Determine if the Relation Could Be a Function.

Yes, the relation could be a function. In order for a relation to be a function, each input value must be assigned exactly one output value. The given points show that the input 3 is assigned 4, and the input 8 is assigned 4. It does not matter that both input values are assigned the same output value. To know for sure if the relation is a function, it must be known that every input value is assigned exactly one output value. Therefore, the relation may or may not be a function.

How Can the X-Intercept Be Determined for a Linear Function Using a Table of Values for the Function?

The x-intercept is the point for which $y = 0$. The x-intercept can be determined for a linear function using a table of values by first checking if the point for which $y = 0$ is in the table. If the table includes the value of x for $y = 0$, then this is the x-intercept. If this value is not in the table, try to determine the value from a pattern in the table. For example, if the y-values for $x = 1$ and $x = 2$ are known, then the difference in these values will also be the difference from $x = 0$ to $x = 1$. If no pattern can be found, calculate the change in the dependent variable divided by the change in the independent variable for two data points. The points can be any two points from the table. Then use the slope and any point from the table to determine the equation for the linear function. Once this is attained, substitute $y = 0$ into the equation and solve for x. The value of x is the x-intercept of the function.

REARRANGE THE EQUATION *AX* + *BY* = *C* TO FIND THE SLOPE *M* OF THE LINE.

To find the slope of the line, write the equation in slope-intercept form, which is $y = mx + b$. When in this form, the coefficient of x is the slope of the line.

$$\begin{aligned} Ax + By &= C \\ By &= -Ax + C \\ y &= \frac{-Ax}{B} + \frac{C}{B} \end{aligned}$$

The coefficient of x is $-\frac{A}{B}$. This is the slope of the line, as long as $B \neq 0$. If $B = 0$, then the equation is of the form $x = \frac{C}{A}$. This is a vertical line, and therefore has undefined slope.

FINDING THE RATE OF CHANGE

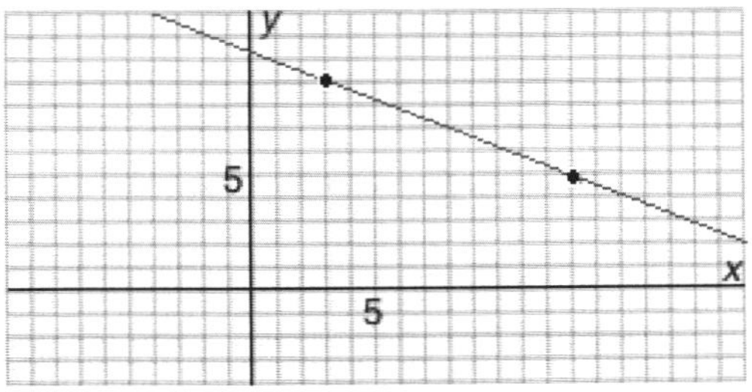

The rate of change can be determined by using any two points from the graph. Two points are given with coordinates (3, 9) and (13, 5). Calculate the slope, or rate of change, by dividing the change in y by the change in x:

$$\frac{9-5}{3-13} = \frac{4}{-10} = -\frac{2}{5}$$

The rate of change is also evident by noting the vertical distance between the points is 4 units, and the horizontal distance is 10 units. However, care must be taken to note the slope is negative, so that the correct rate of change of $-\frac{4}{10} = -\frac{2}{5}$ is determined.

SKETCHING A GRAPH OF A LINEAR FUNCTION THAT IS NEITHER DECREASING NOR INCREASING

A linear function with a positive slope is increasing, and a linear function with a negative slope is decreasing. A linear function that is neither of these must have a slope of 0. This means that the graph of the linear function is a horizontal line. A vertical line has an undefined slope, and also does not represent a function, so the graph cannot be a vertical line. An example of a graph of a horizontal line is shown below. The equation of the line is $y = -2$.

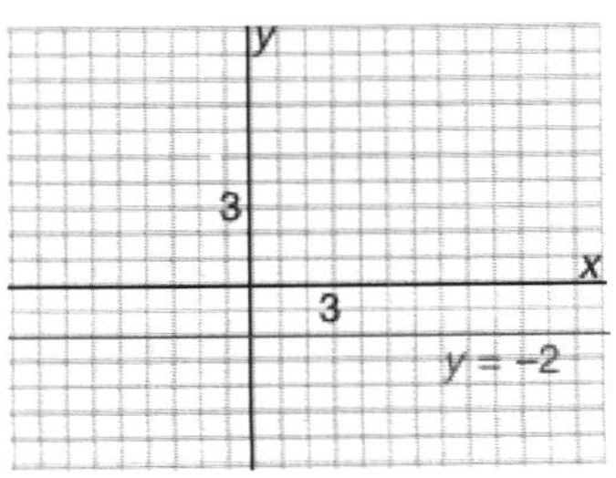

Luis says that a linear function that is rotated in the coordinate plane always results in another linear function. Determine why this is not true.

A linear function represents a line. When a line is rotated it could become vertical. A vertical line is not a function; therefore, a linear function that is rotated in the coordinate plane does not always result in another linear function.

Methods to manually test whether a reflection of an angle in the coordinate plane results in a congruent angle

To manually test if a reflection in the coordinate plane of an angle results in a congruent angle, the angle measures must be compared in some way. The first step would be two draw some triangles in the coordinate plane, and then draw some reflections over different lines. Congruent angles have equal measures. One way to then compare the angle measures would be to measure the angle measures with a protractor. If corresponding angles have the same measure, this would support the claim that angles are taken to angles with the same measure. A second way to compare the angles would be to trace the original triangles on tracing paper. Then flip the paper over, and see if the triangles can be overlaid on top of the reflected triangles.

Line *m* is parallel to line *n*. The lines are translated several units up and several units to the right, forming lines *m´* and *n´*. Name all the pairs of lines that are parallel.

Line *m* and line *n* are parallel. In addition, lines *m´* and *n´* are parallel, because translations take parallel lines to parallel lines. To know whether or not any other combinations of lines are parallel, the number of units of the translation must be known. This is because line *m* may have been taken to itself, or possibly to line *n*. Similarly, line *n* may have been taken to itself, or to line *m*. A line cannot be parallel to itself. As an example, suppose the lines have slope $\frac{2}{3}$. If the translation is up 2 units and right 3 units, each line will be taken to itself.

Segment *AB* has endpoints *A*(−1, 1) and *B*(-1, 4). Use a sequence of transformations to prove segment *AB* is congruent to segment *CD* with endpoints *C*(1, −1) and *D*(4, −1).

The segments are congruent if there is a sequence of rotations, reflections, or translations that take segment *AB* to segment *CD*. Because *AB* is a vertical segment and CD is a horizontal segment, first rotate segment *AB* clockwise 90° about the origin. The gives segment *A´B´* with endpoints *A´*(1, 1) and *B´*(4, 1). Next, translate segment *A´B´* down 2 units. This gives the segment *A´´B´´* with endpoints *A´´*(1, –1) and *B´´* (4, –1). These are the endpoints of segment *CD*, so segment *AB* is therefore congruent to segment *CD*.

Effect on the coordinates of segment *XY* after a reflection over the *y*-axis

After a reflection over the *y*-axis, the *x*-coordinates of the points of segment *XY* are multiplied by –1. This is because each point on *XY* and the corresponding point of the reflection image *X´Y´* are the same distance from the *y*-axis. For example, if point *X* has coordinates X(3, –6), then the image *X´* would have coordinates *X´*(–3, –6). Even if *XY* is on the y-axis, this will work, because the *x*-coordinates of *XY* are equal to 0. This means the x-coordinates will remain 0 when multiplied by –1, and the reflection image *X´Y´* is the same as the original pre-image *XY*.

Yolanda claims that if two figures are similar, then one can be obtained from the first by a sequence of rotations, reflections, and translations. What is wrong with her statement?

Yolanda may be thinking about congruent figures. If two figures are congruent, one can be obtained from the first by a sequence of rotations, reflections, and translations. These congruent figures are also similar. However, if two figures are similar but are not congruent, then the sequence of transformations must also include a dilation. This is because the figures do not have the same size, despite having the same shape. If Yolanda includes dilations in her list of transformations, her statement would be correct: if two figures are similar, then one can be obtained from the first by a sequence of rotations, reflections, translations, and dilations.

Angle-angle criterion for similar triangle and does it apply to congruent triangles

The angle-angle criterion for similar triangles states that two triangles are similar if they have two congruent angles. Angles are congruent if they have the same measure. Triangles have 3 interior angles, and the sum of the measures of the angles is 180°. It follows that if two angle measures are the same in two triangles, then the 3rd angles must also be the same measure. The angle-angle criterion does not apply to congruent triangles. That is, if two triangles have two congruent angles, the triangles are not necessarily congruent, despite the fact that all 3 angles are actually congruent. For example, two equilateral triangles could have sides of 10 units and 20 units. They are not congruent triangles, but they are similar.

Melissa is reading a proof of the Pythagorean Theorem. It begins with the diagram shown. Determine how the figure will use areas to prove the theorem.

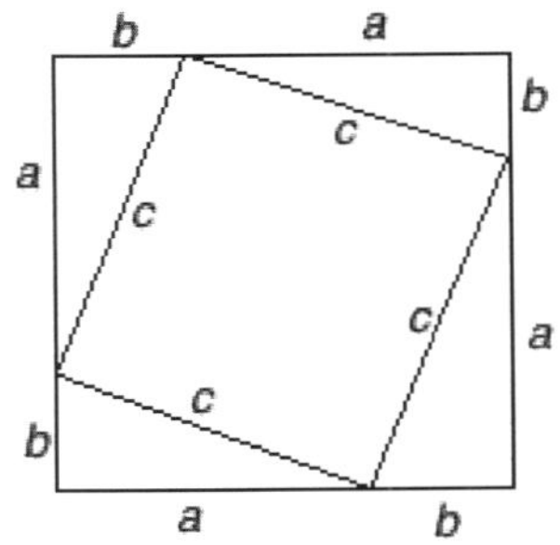

The figure shows a square with side length $a + b$. The square has an inscribed square with side length c, which also is the hypotenuse of 4 congruent right triangles. The figure can be used to write two equivalent expressions for the area of the large square, and then to write an equation to arrive at the Pythagorean Theorem.

Area of large square = $(a + b)^2$

Area of large square = area of small square and

4 triangles = $c^2 + 4 \cdot \frac{1}{2}ab$

$(a + b)^2 = c^2 + 4 \cdot \frac{1}{2}ab$

$a^2 + 2ab + b^2 = c^2 + 2ab$

$a^2 + b^2 = c^2$

A CUBE HAS A SIDE LENGTH OF 10 INCHES. WHAT IS THE DISTANCE FROM ONE CORNER OF THE CUBE TO THE OPPOSITE CORNER?

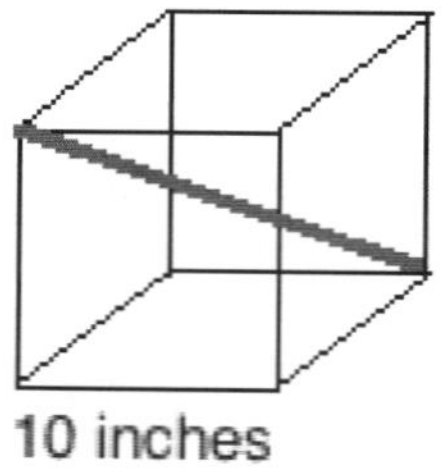

Each face of the cube is a 10-inch square. In order to determine the length of the segment from one corner to the opposite corner, first calculate the diagonal of a face of the cube using the Pythagorean Theorem.

$$10^2 + 10^2 = d^2$$
$$200 = d^2$$
$$d = \sqrt{200} = 10\sqrt{2}$$

The diagonal of the face of the cube, along with an edge of the cube, forms a right triangle with the desired segment as a hypotenuse. This gives the figure shown. Apply the Pythagorean Theorem again to find the length.

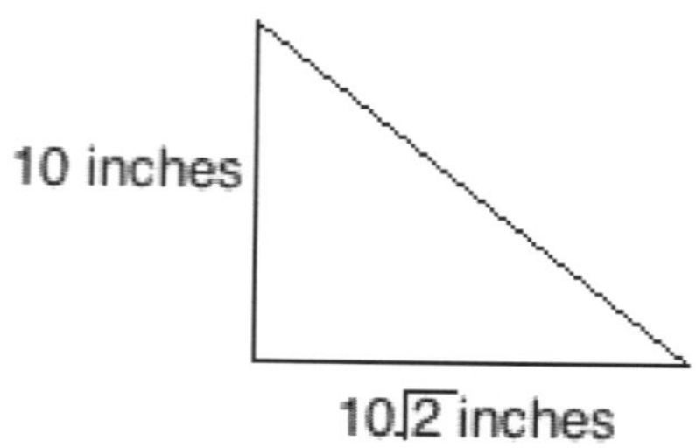

$$10^2 + \left(10\sqrt{2}\right)^2 = c^2$$
$$300 = d^2$$
$$d = \sqrt{300} = 10\sqrt{3}$$

The length from one corner to the opposite corner is $10\sqrt{3}$ inches.

FIND AN EXPRESSION THAT GIVES THE DISTANCE FROM (A, A) TO (B, B), WHERE $A < B$.

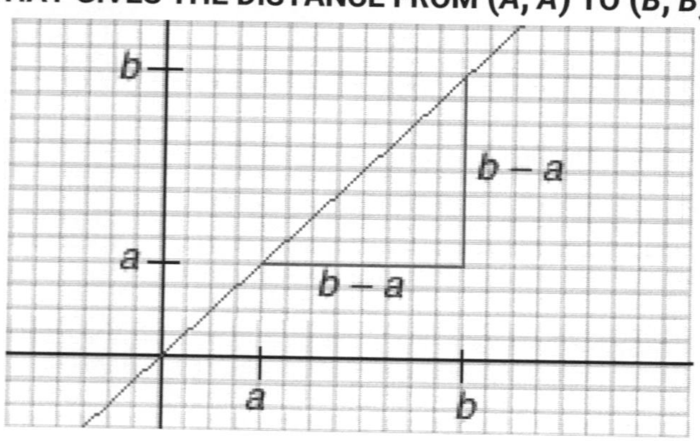

The distance between points (a, a) and (b, b), where $a < b$ is the length of a segment of the line $y = x$. The diagram shows two such points. Since $a < b$, the horizontal distance between the points is $b - a$. Similarly, the vertical distance between the points is $b - a$. The Pythagorean Theorem can be used to find the hypotenuse of the triangle, which is the distance from (a, a) to (b, b).

$$(b - a)^2 + (b - a)^2 = d^2$$

$$2(b - a)^2 = d^2$$

$$d = \sqrt{2(b - a)^2}$$

$$d = \sqrt{2}(b - a)$$

The distance is $\sqrt{2}(b - a)$ units.

Finding the Volume of a Can of Soup with a Radius of 1.5 Inches and a Height of 6 Inches

A can is in the shape of a cylinder. To find the volume of the can with a radius of 1.5 inches and a height of 6 inches, use the formula for the volume of a cylinder, $V = \pi r^2 h$. The variable r represents the radius, which is 1.5 inches, and the variable h represents the height, which is 6 inches. The units for volume will be in cubic inches, since the radius and the height are given in inches.

$$V = \pi r^2 h$$
$$V = \pi(1.5)^2 \cdot 6 = 13.5\pi \approx 42.4$$

The volume of the can of soup is about 42.4 cubic inches.

Clustering in the Context of a Scatter Plot

A scatter plot is a graph that shows data points for bivariate data. The points can be examined to see if there is any relationship between the two variables. Clustering refers to the grouping of several of the data points around a particular value or values of the data set, so much so that the data points appear to form a "cluster" on the graph. This clustering may be an indicator of an additional relationship in the data, such as a preference or most likely event. For example, a scatter plot of "age" and "ice cream cones bought" might show clustering around 25–30 years old and 3–4 ice creams, because an area has many young families with children.

Why a Best-Fit Line May Not Be Reasonable for Data Points Far Beyond the Data in the Graph

There are various reasons why a best-fit line may not be reasonable for data points far beyond the data in the graph. One reason may be limiting factors on one of the variables. For example, a scatter plot of times for a 100-meter race may show a negative linear relationship, but it is unreasonable to assume the times would continue to get faster indefinitely. Another reason may be the changes in other variables that affect the relationship in the data. For example, the cost of a 3-bedroom home may show a positive linear relationship over several years, but then decline for economic reasons.

A SCATTER PLOT SHOWS THE AVERAGE TEMPERATURE (°F) *T* IN AUGUST ON THE HORIZONTAL AXIS, AND THE NUMBER OF TORNADOES *N* IN AUGUST ON THE VERTICAL AXIS. THE BEST-FIT LINE FOR THE DATA IS $N = 0.075T - 4$. WHAT DO THE SLOPE AND *N*-INTERCEPT SUGGEST ABOUT THE DATA?

The slope of the line represents the rate of change in the number of tornadoes per 1 °F temperature change. The slope is 0.075 or $\frac{3}{40}$, which means that for each 40 °F increase in temperature, there is an additional 3 tornadoes. The *n*-intercept is –4, which represents –4 tornadoes for a temperature of 0 °F. These values suggest that the temperature data was probably between 70 °F and 100 °F, because a temperature of almost 70 °F is needed for the best-fit line to get a value of 1 tornado. Similarly, a temperature of over 100 °F would be needed to produce 4 tornadoes.

THE TABLE SHOWS THE RESULTS FOR A VOTE ON WHETHER THE SCHOOL MASCOT SHOULD BE CHANGED. DESCRIBE HOW TO MAKE A RELATIVE FREQUENCY TABLE FOR THE ROWS.

	Yes	**No**
Girls	36	24
Boys	48	12

To make a relative frequency table, calculate the relative frequencies for each group. Adding the frequencies shows that there are 24 + 36 = 60 girls and 48 + 12 = 60 boys that voted. The relative frequencies for the rows, or the girls and the boys, are calculated as follows:

Voted yes and is a girl: $\frac{36}{60} = 0.6$ Voted no and is a girl: $\frac{24}{60} = 0.4$

Voted yes and is a boy: $\frac{48}{60} = 0.8$ Voted no and is a boy: $\frac{12}{60} = 0.2$

	Yes	**No**	**Total**
Girls	0.6	0.4	1
Boys	0.8	0.2	1

The relative frequency table is shown, with the sums of the rows having a sum of 1.

RATIONAL NUMBERS

All decimal numbers that repeat a pattern or terminate (which can also be thought of as repeating zeros) are rational numbers. The definition of a rational number is any number that can be written as a ratio of two integers. To show 3.125 can be written in this form, covert the decimal 0.125 to a fraction. Since there are 3 digits after the decimal, begin by writing 0.125 as 125 over 1000:

$$\mathbf{0.125 = \frac{125}{1000} = \frac{5}{40} = \frac{1}{8}}$$

The number 3.125 is therefore equal to the mixed fraction $3\frac{1}{8}$. Convert this fraction to an improper fraction:

$$3\frac{1}{8} = \frac{25}{8}$$

The rational number 3.125 is written as a ratio of two integers as $\frac{25}{8}$.

If n is a positive integer and n < 100, when is $\sqrt[3]{\boldsymbol{n}}$ rational? The expression $\sqrt[3]{n}$ represents the cube root of the number *n*. This means that if $a = \sqrt[3]{n}$, then $a^3 = n$. For the expression $\sqrt[3]{n}$ to be a rational number, n must be a perfect cube. A perfect cube is the cube of an integer, such as 27: $27 = 3^3$. To find the perfect cubes that are less than 100, it is easiest to cube the integers 1, 2, 3,... until the cube is greater than 99.

$1^3 = 1, 2^3 = 8, 3^3 = 27, 4^3 = 64, 5^3 = 125$

The expression $\sqrt[3]{n}$ is rational for $n < 100$ when n is 1, 8, 27, or 64.

Using the approximation $\sqrt{2} \approx 1.41$ to compare the numbers $3\sqrt{2}$ and $\frac{21}{5}$

The irrational number $3\sqrt{2}$ is equal to 3 times the number $\sqrt{2}$. Use the given approximation for $\sqrt{2}$ to write a decimal approximation for $3\sqrt{2}$:

$$3\sqrt{2} = 3 \cdot \sqrt{2} \approx 3 \cdot 1.41 = 4.23$$

The number 4.23 is a rational number approximation for the irrational number $3\sqrt{2}$. To compare this to the fraction $\frac{21}{5}$, either convert the fraction to a decimal or convert the decimal approximation to a fraction. It is easy to convert the fraction to a decimal: $\frac{21}{5} = 4\frac{1}{5} = 4.2$, or 4.20. This is slightly less than the number 4.23, so $\frac{21}{5} < 3\sqrt{2}$.

Effect of Zero as an Exponent Using a Property of Integer Exponents

For any non-zero number a, the expression $a^0 = 1$. If the base $a = 0$, then the expression is undefined. This meaning of zero as an exponent makes sense for all of the properties of integer exponents. For example, when multiplying two exponential expressions with the same base, the exponents are added: $a^m a^n = a^{m+n}$. If $m = 0$, then the expression would look like this:

$$a^0 a^n = a^{0+n} = a^n$$

This equation says $a^0 a^n = a^n$, which must mean that $a^0 = 1$. Similar justifications are possible for the other properties of integer exponents.

Expressing the Number 5,000,000,000,000,000 as a Single Digit Times an Integer Power of 10

To write the number 5,000,000,000,000,000 as a single digit times an integer power of 10, first examine some integer powers of 10:

$10^{-3} = 0.001$	$10^2 = 100$
$10^{-2} = 0.01$	$10^3 = 1{,}000$
$10^{-1} = 0.1$	$10^4 = 10{,}000$
$10^0 = 0$	$10^5 = 100{,}000$
$10^1 = 1$	$10^6 = 1{,}000{,}000$

The pattern shows that for positive integer powers of 10, when the exponent is n then the number is written as 1 followed by n zeros. The number 5,000,000,000,000,000 = 5 × 1,000,000,000,000,000, which has a 1 followed by 15 zeros as a factor. It follows that the number 5,000,000,000,000,000 can be written as 5×10^{15}, which is a digit times an integer power of 10.

Dividing Small Numbers Written in Scientific Notation

When dividing very small numbers in scientific notation, divide the coefficients (the numbers multiplied by a power of 10) and the powers of 10 separately. That is, $\frac{a\times10^m}{b\times10^n}=\frac{a}{b}\cdot10^m10^n$. In this way, the exponent property $\frac{a^m}{a^n}=a^{m-n}$ can be applied to the powers of 10, leaving only one power of 10. If the quotient $\frac{a}{b}$ is not between 1 and 10, then adjust the expression so that the result is also in scientific notation:

$$\frac{7.80\times10^{-23}}{9.75\times10^{-19}}=\frac{7.80}{9.75}\cdot\frac{10^{-23}}{10^{-19}}=0.8\times10^{-4}=8.0\times10^{-5}$$

Note that $0.8=8.0\times10^{-1}$, which explains why $0.8\times10^{-4}=8.0\times10^{-5}$.

A DVD Service Charges a $50 Sign-Up Fee and $10/Month for Unlimited DVDs. Is the Graph of Total Cost as a Function of Number of Months a Graph of a Proportional Relationship?

It is not a proportional relationship because of the sign-up fee. If y is proportional to x, then $y = kx$, where k is a non-zero constant. The DVD service charge; however, starts out with a $50 service charge (at zero months) and then increases $10 per month. The equation of this line is $y = 10x + 50$. 50 is added to the right side of the equation regardless of the value of x; therefore, the right side of the equation is not proportional to the left. Note that the line representing a proportional relationship passes through the origin where x and y both equal zero. If the DVD service did not charge a sign-up fee, it would be a proportional relationship.

Derive the Equation $y = mx$ for a Non-Vertical Line Through the Origin, Where the Slope m Is the Change in y Divided by the Change in x for Any Two Points on the Graph.

Graph a straight line through the origin (0, 0). Any point (x, y) on the line will be x units from the y-axis and y units from the x-axis, as is illustrated in the diagram. This will even be true for a horizontal line—each point will be x units from the y-axis and 0 units from the x-axis (the line *is* the x-axis).

The slope is the ratio of the change in y and the change in x, so write an equation for the slope: $m=\frac{y}{x}$, for any point (x, y) on the graph. Solving this equation for y gives $y = mx$.

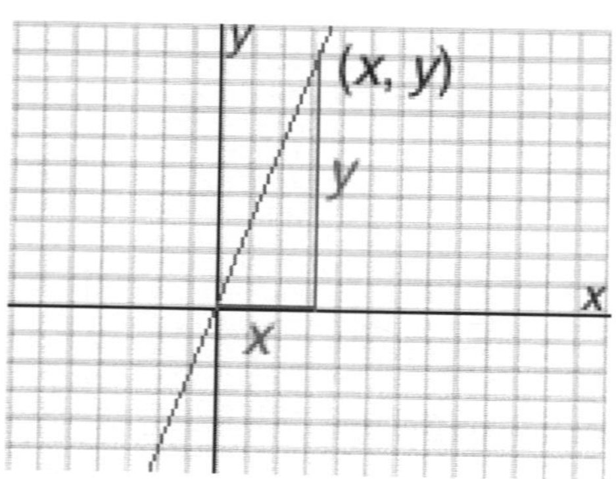

Finding the Value(s) of b Such That $2x + 4 = b(x + 1)$

To find the value(s) of b, first solve the equation for x:

$$2x+4=b(x+1)$$

$$2x + 4 = bx + b$$
$$2x - bx = b - 4$$
$$x(2 - b) = b - 4$$
$$x = \frac{b - 4}{2 - b}$$

The expression for x is undefined for $b = 2$.

It follows that the equation $2x + 4 = b(x + 1)$ has one solution and $b \neq 2$.

How a Least Common Denominator Can Help to Solve Linear Equations with Fractions and Fractional Coefficients

When solving a linear equation with fractions and fractional coefficients, a least common denominator or LCD can simplify the operations. By multiplying each side of the equation by the LCD, the denominators of the fractions are cleared out. This results in a linear equation that has integers and integer coefficients, and it is easier to solve for the variable. This is illustrated in the following example:

$$\frac{2}{3}x + \frac{1}{5} = -x + \frac{5}{6}$$
$$30\left(\frac{2}{3}x + \frac{1}{5}\right) = 30\left(-x + \frac{5}{6}\right)$$
$$20x + 6 = -30x + 25$$
$$50x = 19$$
$$x = \frac{19}{50}$$

Ryan Says the Solution to the System $x + y = 4$ and $2x - y = -7$ is $(3, 1)$. Determine if This Is Correct or Incorrect.

A solution to a system of two linear equations is a point (x, y) that satisfies both equations of the system. In this case, Ryan found an incorrect solution because the point $(3, 1)$ only satisfies the equation $x + y = 4$. When $x = 3$ and $y = 1$ are substituted into the equation $2x - y = -7$, the result is $5 = -7$, which is false. The correct solution to the system is the point $(-1, 5)$:

$x + y = 4$	$2x - y = -7$
$-1 + 5 = 4$	$2(-1) - (5) = -7$
$4 = 4$	$-7 = -7$

Note that there are an infinite number of solutions for either of the two equations, but only one solution for the system. This solution point corresponds to the intersection point of the graphs of the equations.

Using Mental Math to Solve the System $2x = 1$ and $y + x = 1$

To solve a system of two linear equations using mental math or by inspection, first try to determine if either of the two equations can be solved right away. In this case, the first equation only has one variable, x. It is also a one-step equation, and is easily solved by dividing each side of the equation by 2. This results in $x = \frac{1}{2}$. The second equation states that the sum of x and y is equal to 1. It must be that $y = \frac{1}{2}$, because $\frac{1}{2} + \frac{1}{2} = 1$. This means the solution of the linear system is $\left(\frac{1}{2}, \frac{1}{2}\right)$.

WRITE A SYSTEM THAT COULD BE USED TO DETERMINE IF AND WHERE THE LINE THROUGH THE ORIGIN AND (3, 2) INTERSECTS THE LINE THROUGH (1, 5) AND (−3, 6).

Find equations for each line. The slope of the first line is

$m = \frac{2-0}{3-0} = \frac{2}{3}$. Use the point-slope form of a line to find the equation:

$$y - y_0 = m(x - x_0)$$
$$y - 0 = \frac{2}{3}(x - 0)$$
$$y = \frac{2}{3}x$$

The slope of the second line is $m = \frac{6-5}{-3-1} = -\frac{1}{4}$. Use the point-slope form of a line to find the equation:

$$y - y_0 = m(x - x_0)$$
$$y - 5 = -\frac{1}{4}(x - 1)$$
$$y = -\frac{1}{4}x + \frac{21}{4}$$

Since the slopes of the two lines are different, they do intersect. The system $y = \frac{2}{3}x$ and $y = -\frac{1}{4}x + \frac{21}{4}$ can be used to determine the point of intersection.

A COMPUTER TAKES AN INPUT FROM THE SET {1, 2, 3}. THE OUTPUT IS A NUMBER FROM {0, 1, 2, 3} THAT IS LESS THAN THE INPUT NUMBER. IS THIS SET OF ALL POSSIBLE PAIRS OF INPUTS AND OUTPUTS A FUNCTION?

A function is a relation such that each input value is assigned exactly one output value. If the computer takes the input 1, only one number in the output set is less than 1, the number 0. However, for any other input, there are multiple possible output values. For example, if the input is 2, then the numbers 0 and 1 are possible outputs. This means that (2, 0) and (2, 1) are in the set of all possible pairs of inputs and outputs. For this reason, the set of all possible pairs of inputs and outputs is not a function.

COMPANY A INCREASES SALES BY 30% EACH YEAR SINCE 2010. COMPANY B HAS YEARLY SALES DESCRIBED BY THE FUNCTION *S* = 14,000 + 6,000*T*, WHERE *T* IS THE NUMBER OF YEARS SINCE 2010. COMPARE THE SALES GROWTH OF THE COMPANIES.

We don't know how much Company A's sales are, but we know that they increase by an amount equal to 30% of the prior year's sales for each year after 2010. Company B on the other hand has \$14,000 in sales in 2010, and an additional \$6,000 in sales for each succeeding year. So its sales growth percentage, rounded to the nearest percent, is as follows:

$$\text{2011 Sales Growth \%} = \frac{\text{2011 Sales Growth}}{\text{2010 Sales}} = \frac{6{,}000}{14{,}000} = 43\%$$

$$\text{2012 Sales Growth \%} = \frac{\text{2012 Sales Growth}}{\text{2011 Sales}} = \frac{6{,}000}{20{,}000} = 30\%$$

$$\text{2013 Sales Growth \%} = \frac{\text{2013 Sales Growth}}{\text{2012 Sales}} = \frac{6{,}000}{26{,}000} = 24\%$$

$$2014 \text{ Sales Growth } \% = \frac{2014 \text{ Sales Growth}}{2013 \text{ Sales}} = \frac{6{,}000}{32{,}000} = 19\%$$

So Company B's Growth % starts out higher than Company A's, but then becomes less.

Jill is given two points of a function. She graphs the points. Because she can draw a straight line through the two points, she decides the function is linear. Explain Jill's error.

Jill did not graph enough points to determine if the graph is linear. In fact, there is a straight line through any two distinct points on the coordinate plane. If a function represents a linear relationship, then all points of the function will fall on the same straight line. If Jill had at least graphed 3 points, she may have been able to determine if the function is *not* linear. This would be evident by all 3 points not lying on a straight line. Note, however, that no matter how many points are graphed and fall on a straight line, it is still possible that the function is not linear.

What is the rate of change of the linear function?

The data in the table represent a linear function. For a linear function, the rate of change is equal to the slope. To find the slope, calculate the change in *y* divided by the change in *x* for any two points from the table:

x	y
3	8
-1	14
-3	17

$$m = \frac{14 - 8}{-1 - 3} = \frac{6}{-4} = -\frac{3}{2}$$

Note that this value is the same for any two points from the table:

$$m = \frac{17 - 8}{-3 - 3} = \frac{9}{-6} = -\frac{3}{2}$$

The rate of change of the linear function is $-\frac{3}{2}$. Remember to subtract in the same direction for the *y*-values and *x*-values. This ensures the correct sign of the rate of change. For example, if the difference −1 – 3 above were written as

3 – (−1) = 4, the slope would have come out to be $\frac{3}{2}$.

A GRAPH OF A FUNCTION IS SHOWN. IS IT LINEAR OR NONLINEAR? WHEN IS THE FUNCTION INCREASING OR DECREASING?

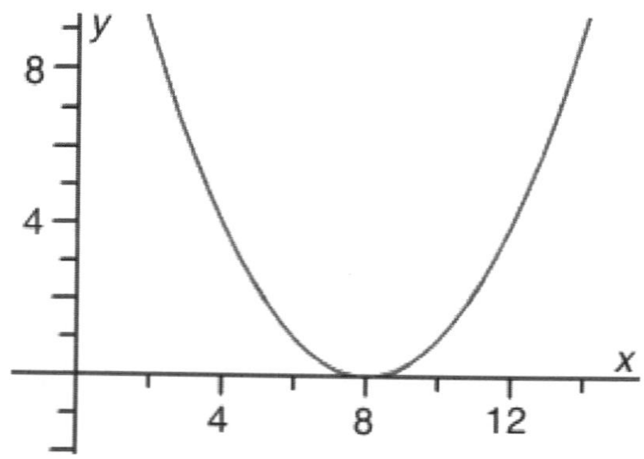

The function is nonlinear. If the function were linear, all of the points would fall in a straight line, resulting in a line graph. Any graph that is curved represents a nonlinear function. The function is increasing when the graph rises from left to right. Similarly, the function is decreasing when the graph falls from left to right. The graph appears to change from decreasing to increasing at the point (8, 0). This means that for $x < 8$, the function is decreasing. For $x > 8$, the function is increasing.

A RIGHT TRIANGLE IN THE COORDINATE PLANE HAS A HYPOTENUSE WITH LENGTH 20 UNITS. THE TRIANGLE IS TRANSLATED 5 UNITS DOWN. WHAT IS THE LENGTH OF THE HYPOTENUSE OF THE TRANSLATED TRIANGLE?

A two-dimensional figure is congruent to another if the second can be obtained from the first by a sequence of rotations, reflections, and translations. The triangle was translated, so the resulting triangle is congruent to the original triangle. Congruent figures have corresponding parts that are congruent, so the hypotenuses of the two triangles are congruent. This means that the length of the hypotenuse of the translated triangle is also 20 units. Note that the distance and direction that the triangle is translated in has no effect on the length of the hypotenuse, or any of the sides of the triangle.

DESCRIBE THE EFFECT ON THE COORDINATES OF A POINT OF A FIGURE IF THE FIGURE IS ROTATED 90° CLOCKWISE ABOUT THE ORIGIN.

When a figure is rotated 90° clockwise about the origin, each point (x, y) is taken to the point $(y, -x)$. This is illustrated by the points (−4, −7) and (5, 2) in the diagram, which are taken to (−7, 4) and (2, −5) respectively. This could further be illustrated using points on the x-axis or y-axis. For example, the point (5, 0) will be taken to the point (0, −5), and the point (10, 0) will be taken to the point (0, −10). Points on the x-axis are taken to the y-axis, and vice-versa.

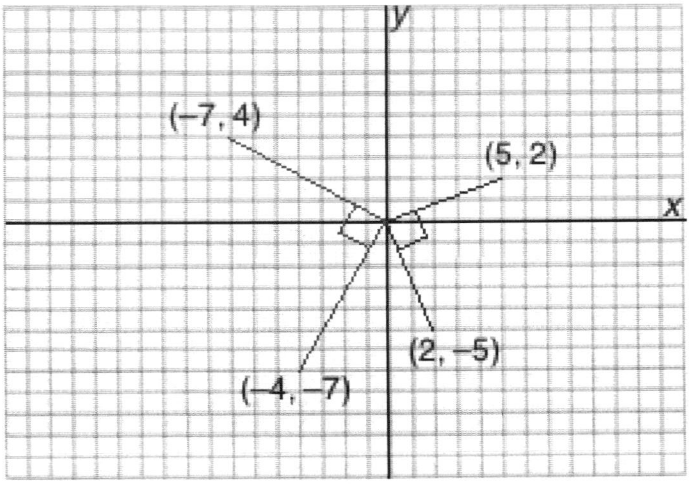

IS THE RECTANGLE WITH VERTICES $A(0, 0)$, $B(0, 4)$, $C(3, 4)$, AND $D(3, 0)$ SIMILAR TO THE RECTANGLE WITH VERTICES $F(0, 0)$, $G(0, 6)$, $H(4.5, 6)$, AND $I(4.5, 0)$?

Yes, the two rectangles are similar figures. A two-dimensional figure is similar to another if the second can be obtained from the first by a sequence of rotations, reflections, translations, and dilations. Each coordinate of the vertices of rectangle *ABCD* was multiplied by 1.5 to get each coordinate of the vertices of rectangle *FGHI*. This means that rectangle *FGHI* is a dilation of rectangle *ABCD* by a factor of 1.5. Another way to verify the figures are similar is to note that both rectangles have 4 congruent right angles, and the ratios of corresponding side lengths are equal.

A TRIANGLE HAS ANGLE MEASURES AS FOLLOWS: $m\angle A = a°$, $m\angle B = b°$, AND $m\angle C = c°$. WRITE AN EXPRESSION FOR THE MEASURE OF THE EXTERIOR ANGLE AT ANGLE A.

An expression for the measure of the exterior angle at angle A is (b + c)°. The sum of the measures of the interior angles of any triangle is 180°. This means that a + b + c = 180. Now let x = the measure of the exterior angle at angle A. Because the exterior angle and angle A form a linear pair, the sum of the measures of these angles is 180°. This means that x + a = 180. Substitution gives the equation x + a = a + b + c, and therefore x = b + c.

A triangle has side lengths of 3 cm, $\sqrt{5}$ cm, and $\sqrt{14}$ cm. Is the triangle a right triangle?

The converse of the Pythagorean Theorem states that if the sum of the squares of the lengths of any two sides of a triangle are equal to the square of the length of the remaining side, then the triangle is a right triangle. For the given lengths to satisfy this statement, the longest length, or $\sqrt{14}$ cm, must be the hypotenuse. 3 cm and $\sqrt{5}$ cm are the lengths of the legs. Check to see if the statement is true:

$$(3)^2 + \left(\sqrt{5}\right)^2 = \left(\sqrt{14}\right)^2$$

$$9 + 5 = 14$$

$$14 = 14$$

The equation is true, so the triangle is a right triangle.

AN ISOSCELES RIGHT TRIANGLE HAS A HYPOTENUSE OF 10 UNITS. WHAT IS THE AREA OF THE TRIANGLE?

An isosceles right triangle has congruent leg lengths. Apply the Pythagorean Theorem, which states that the sum of the squares of the lengths of the legs is equal to the square of the length of the hypotenuse:

$a^2 + b^2 = c^2$	Pythagorean Theorem
$b^2 + b^2 = 10^2$	The legs are congruent, so use b for each leg length.
$2b^2 = 100$	
$b^2 = 50$	
$b = \sqrt{50}$	

The area of the triangle is one half the base times the height, or in this case $A = \frac{1}{2}b^2$, where $b^2 = 50$. The area of the triangle is therefore 25 square units.

USE THE PYTHAGOREAN THEOREM TO FIND THE LENGTH OF SEGMENT *RU*.

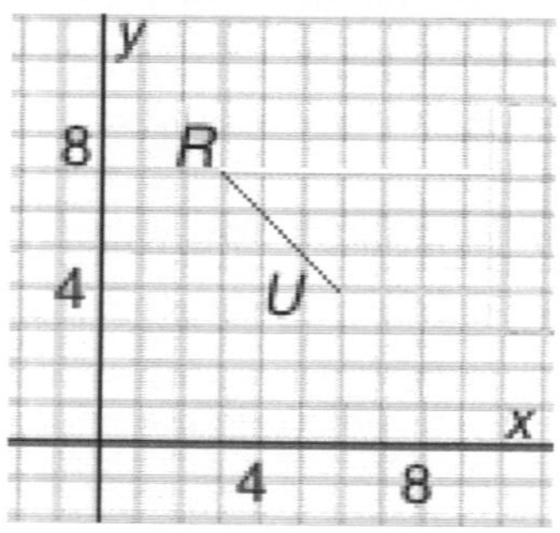

First, identify the coordinates of points R and U. Point R has coordinates $R(3, 7)$ and point U has coordinates $U(6, 4)$. To apply the Pythagorean Theorem, draw a vertical segment down from point R and a horizontal segment left from point U to form a right triangle with RU as its hypotenuse. The lengths of the legs of the triangle are the difference between the x-coordinates and the difference between the y-coordinates of points R and U:

vertical leg length = 7 – 4 = 3 units

horizontal leg length = 6 – 3 = 3 units

By the Pythagorean Theorem, the length of segment RU is $\sqrt{3^2 + 3^2} = \sqrt{18}$ units.

Similarities Between the Formulas for the Volume of a Cylinder and the Volume of a Cone

The formula for the volume of a cylinder is $V = \pi r^2 h$, where r is the radius of the circular base and h is the height. The formula for the volume of a cone is $V = \frac{1}{3}\pi r^2 h$, where r is the radius of the circular base and h is the height. This means that a cone that has the same circular base and height as a cylinder has exactly one third the volume of the cylinder. If the cone were placed inside the cylinder, it would occupy one third of the interior space.

Outlier of a Data Set

An outlier of a data set is a data point that is very far from most of the data points. A data set may have more than one outlier, but there should not be many, as then the supposed outliers may actually be representative of the population. In general, when a sample of data is taken from a population, it is best to throw away outliers before making any conclusions about the data. An outlier could be the result of an error. For example, if various measures were taken with a 60-inch tape measure, and most values were around 39 inches, a value of 21 inches is likely from the measurer misreading the tape measure.

Knowing When a Scatter Plot Suggests a Linear Association

The phrase "suggests a linear association" means that the data appear to show a pattern that follows a straight line. This means that a best-fit line should function as a good predictor for data points that fall between given data, or beyond the given data. It does not mean that the data points actually fall on a line, only that the points are all close to a line. The line may have a positive or negative slope, or even appear horizontal or vertical. Data that does not show a linear correlation may show no correlation, which means the points appear to be dispersed randomly on the graph. Alternatively, the data may show some other type of association, such as a quadratic or exponential association. Such data points will appear to follow a curve that is not straight.

A Scatter Plot Shows the Money Spent at a Mall as a Function of the Time Spent in the Mall for Several Customers. Interpret the Meaning of a Positive or Negative Slope for the Best-Fit Line of the Data.

Suppose the scatter plot of the money spent at a mall as a function of the time spent in the mall has a best-fit line with a positive slope. This means that the more time spent at the mall, the more a customer spends at the mall. This may mean customers are spending a lot of time comparing expensive items before finally making a purchase. If, on the other hand, the slope is negative, then the more time spent at the mall, the less a customer spends. This means that customers come to the mall with a purpose to buy something and then leave, or are hanging out and not spending much money at all. In either case, the slope represents money spent per hour, described as a rate of change.

MILLIE IS WATCHING STUDENTS OPEN AND GO THROUGH A SET OF DOUBLE DOORS AT THE SCHOOL. HER DATA IS SHOWN IN THE TABLE.

	Left Door	Right Door
Left Hand	28	13
Right Hand	50	78

The data in the table shows that most students will open the door on the right when they approach the double doors. This is because 13 + 78 = 91 students open the right door, whereas 28 + 50 = 78 open the left door. A greater difference than this is seen in which hand is used to open the door. Over 3 times as many students open the door with the right hand, because 50 + 78 = 128 and 28 + 13 = 41. Overall, most students elect to open the right door with the right hand, because 78 is the greatest entry in the table.

IS THE PRODUCT OF TWO IRRATIONAL NUMBERS ALWAYS IRRATIONAL ?

The product of two irrational numbers is NOT always irrational. It is easiest to prove a statement like this as false by finding a counterexample. If there is even one pair of irrational numbers that multiply to be a rational number, then this disproves the statement. Consider the irrational number $\sqrt{2}$. When the number is multiplied by itself, the result is 2: $\sqrt{2} \cdot \sqrt{2} = 2$. The number 2 is a rational number, because it can be written as $\frac{2}{1}$, which is a ratio of integers. In fact, if $\sqrt{n}$ is irrational for some positive integer n, then multiplying this number by itself always results in the rational number n.

The numbers 3.14 and $\frac{22}{7}$ can be used to approximate π. Which is more accurate?

In order to determine which number is a more accurate representation of the irrational number π, first write π to several decimal places, using a calculator:

$$\pi = 3.141592 \ldots$$

To make the comparison, next write the number $\frac{22}{7}$ as a decimal, so that all three values are written in decimal form:

$$\frac{22}{7} = 3.\overline{142857}$$

Write the decimals in order in a column, to better examine them:

3.140000

3.141592

3.142857

The approximations begin to differ from π in the 3rd decimal place, but both differences are 0.001, so it's not yet apparent which approximation is closest. If the 4th decimal place is included, the differences become 0.0015 and 0.0013. Therefore $\frac{22}{7}$ is a better approximation.

IF N IS A POSITIVE INTEGER, ARE $(-3)^N$ AND -3^N EQUIVALENT EXPRESSIONS?

To evaluate $(-3)^n$ and -3^n, both the properties of integer exponents and the order of operations must be used. Since expressions in parentheses are evaluated first, the expression $(-3)^n$ represents a product of n factors of −3, and the result will be either positive or negative depending on whether n is even or odd. The expression -3^n, however, must have the exponent evaluated first. So, the expression -3^n is always negative. Since $(-3)^n$ is only negative for odd values of n the two expressions are equivalent only for odd values of n.

If n is a positive integer and $3n < 100$, for what values of n is $\sqrt{3n}$ rational?

$\sqrt{3n}$ is rational when $3n$ is a perfect square. The perfect squares that are less than 100 are: 1, 4, 9, 25, 36, 49, 64, and 81. Since n is an integer, the possible values for n are 3, 12, and 27. It can also be noted that in order for $3n$ to be a perfect square, n must be 3 times a perfect square. Therefore, possible values of n are:

$n = 3(1^2) = 3$
$n = 3(2^2) = 12$
$n = 3(3^2) = 27$

The expression $\sqrt{3n}$ is rational for $3n < 100$ when n is 3, 12, or 27.

AN *ASTRONOMICAL UNIT* IS A UNIT OF LENGTH EQUAL TO ABOUT 149,597,871 KILOMETERS. ESTIMATE THIS LENGTH BY WRITING IT AS A SINGLE DIGIT TIMES A POWER OF 10.

To estimate 149,597,871 kilometers as a single digit times a power of 10, first determine the power of 10. A single digit means an integer from 1 to 9, so the decimal place must move to the left until the value of the number is between 1 and 10. For 149,597,871, move 8 places: 1.49597871. Now multiply this number times 10^8 to make up for moving the decimal 8 places to the left:

$149{,}597{,}871 = 1.49597871 \times 10^8$. Finally, to estimate with a single digit, we round 1.49597871 down to 1, because $4 < 5$. This gives

1×10^8.

CAN THE PRODUCT $(3.5 \times 10^9)(4.0 \times 101^2)$ BE SIMPLIFIED USING THE DISTRIBUTIVE PROPERTY? IF NOT, WHAT PROPERTIES CAN BE USED?

No, the product $(3.5 \times 10^9)(4.0 \times 10^{12})$ cannot be simplified using the distributive property. The distributive property is used when one of the factors in a product involves the sum or difference of two or more terms. The given product only involves multiplication, and could be written without parentheses as follows:

$\mathbf{3.5 \times 10^9 \times 4.0 \times 10^{12}}$

The order of the factors can then be rearranged by applying the commutative property of multiplication. Then the associative property of multiplication allows multiplying the powers of 10 and the other numbers separately:

$\mathbf{3.5 \times 10^9 \times 4.0 \times 10^{12} =}$
$\mathbf{3.5 \times 4.0 \times 10^9 \times 10^{12} =}$ **Commutative Property**
$(3.5 \times 4.0) \times (10^9 \times 10^{12}) =$ Associative Property

$14 \times 10^{21} = 1.4 \times 10^{22}$ Add exponents, write in scientific notation.

IF 7 POUNDS OF BANANAS COST $5.53, WHAT IS THE UNIT RATE? HOW DOES IT RELATE TO A GRAPH THAT DESCRIBES THIS RELATIONSHIP?

A rate is a ratio that relates one unit to another. This rate is a unit rate when the denominator is equal to 1. If 7 pounds of bananas cost $5.53, then the rate is $5.53 per 7 pounds of bananas.

Dividing gives the unit rate: 5.53 ÷ 7 = 0.79, so the unit rate is \$.79 per pound. Note that a fraction can still describe a unit rate. For example, a rate of $\frac{3}{4}$ mile per minute is a unit rate, because the rate is per 1 minute.

The slope of the graph representing the cost of several pounds of bananas is equal to the unit rate. This is because the slope

$m = \frac{\text{change in cost}}{\text{change in bananas}}$ for any two points on the graph, which will always give 0.79.

Derive the Equation $y = mx + b$ for a Non-Vertical Line, Where m Is the Slope and b Is the y-Intercept.

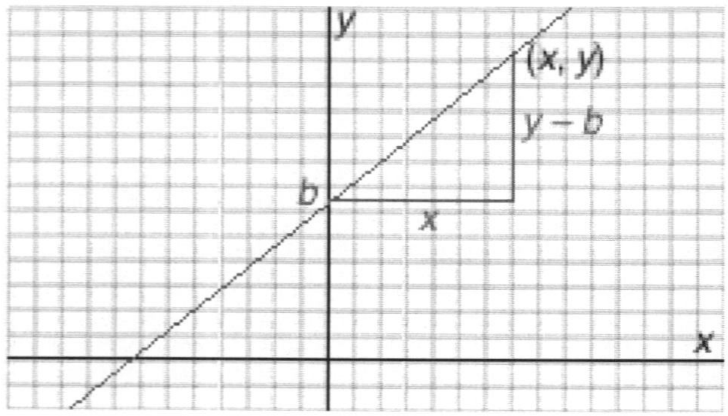

Graph a straight line through the point (0, b). Draw a right triangle with a point (x, y) on the line and (0, b) as the endpoints of the hypotenuse, as is illustrated in the diagram. The leg lengths of the triangle are therefore x and $y - b$.

The slope is the ratio of the change in y and the change in x, so write an equation for the slope: $m = \frac{y-b}{x}$, for any point (x, y) on the graph. Solving this equation for y gives $y = mx + b$. Note that for a horizontal line, $y - b = 0$ which simply gives the equation $y = b$.

Find the Value(s) of b Such That $3x - 2b = 3x + 3$ Has All Real Numbers as Its Solution

To find the value(s) of b, first solve the equation for x:

$$3x - 2b = 3x + 3$$

$$-2b = 3$$

The x-terms of the equation have cancelled out. When this happens, if the resulting equation is false, there is no solution. If the resulting equation is true, then all real numbers is the solution. Since all real numbers is the desired solution, solve the equation to find the value of b that makes the equation true:

$$\begin{aligned} -2b &= 3 \\ b &= -\frac{3}{2} \end{aligned}$$

The equation has all real numbers as its solution when $b = -\frac{3}{2}$. Notice that the equation becomes $3x + 3 = 3x + 3$, which is an identity. For any value of x, each side of the equation is equal to 3.

RATIONAL NUMBER COEFFICIENT

A coefficient is the real number factor of a variable term. For example, in the term $-3x^3y^2$ and the term $10b$, the coefficients are –3 and 10, respectively. A rational number coefficient is a coefficient that is a rational number, which is a number than can be written as a ratio of two integers. –3 and 10 are therefore examples of rational number coefficients. In the term $x\sqrt{2}$, the coefficient $\sqrt{2}$ is not a rational number, so $\sqrt{2}$ is not a rational number coefficient. When like terms with rational number coefficients are combined, it is the rational number coefficients that are added or subtracted, keeping the same variable component. For example, $3x + 7x = (3 + 7)x = 10x$. The same is true when combining like terms with irrational number coefficients.

ILENE SAYS THE LINEAR SYSTEM REPRESENTING BY THE GRAPH HAS NO SOLUTION. EXPLAIN ILENE'S ERROR.

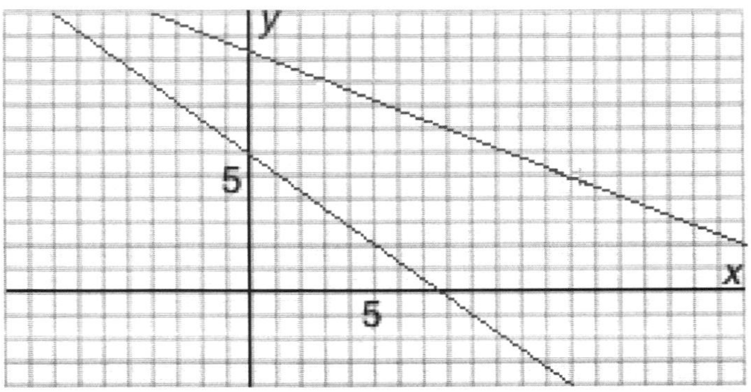

Ilene assumed that because the lines do not have a visible intersection point on the graph, the lines do not intersect. When a linear system is graphed and the lines do not intersect, or are parallel, then the system has no solution. However, it is clear from the graph that the lines will intersect, and that the lines are not parallel. The intersection point will be in the second quadrant. To find the solution of the system, either another graph is needed that shows the intersection point, or the equations for the lines can be used to find the solution algebraically. Note that even lines that appear to be parallel may not be. The slopes must be proven to be equal to know the lines are parallel.

HOW THE SYSTEM $x - 2y = -4$ AND $x + 2y = 6$ CAN BE SOLVED BY ADDING THE EQUATIONS TOGETHER

The solution to a linear system of two equations must make both equations true. Two true equations when added together form a 3rd true equation. For example, 3 = 3 and 8 = 8, so it follows that 3 + 8 = 3 + 8. Write the equations vertically and add them:

$$\begin{aligned} x - 2y &= -4 \\ \underline{x + 2y} &\underline{= 6 +} \\ 2x &= 2 \\ x &= 1 \end{aligned}$$

The y-terms cancel, which gives the equation $2x = 2$, so $x = 1$. Substitute 1 for x in either of the original equations to see that $y = 2.5$. The solution is (1, 2.5).

HOW A SYSTEM OF TWO NON-PARALLEL LINEAR EQUATIONS THAT IS INTENDED TO REPRESENT A REAL-WORLD SITUATION MIGHT HAVE NO VALID SOLUTION.

When a real-world situation is represented by a system of two linear equations, the system can be mathematically solved, but care must be taken to make sure the solution makes sense in the context of the problem. For example, a value that represents the number of people at a concert cannot be 480.5, and a value that represents the distance across a river cannot be –20. When this happens, it means that there is no valid solution to the problem, even if the system has a correct numerical solution. Of course, if a legitimate solution is expected, check to make sure the system was both written correctly and solved correctly.

Ray says that $Y = X^2$ is not a function. This is because $X = 2$ gives $Y = 4$ and $X = -2$ gives $Y = 4$. Is Ray correct?

Ray is not correct. A function is a rule that assigns to each input exactly one output. In Ray's example, the input 2 is assigned the output 4, and the input –2 is assigned the output 4. This does not contradict the definition of a function. In order to find an example to show $y = x^2$ is not a function, Ray would have to find an x-value that gives two different y-values, which he cannot do for $y = x^2$.

A function takes an input, adds 1, then doubles the result. Another function is described by the equation $Y = 2X + 2$

In order to compare these functions, determine the algebraic equation that represents the verbal description "takes an input, adds 1, then doubles the result." First, begin with the function $y = x$, where x is the input. Then add 1: $y = x + 1$. Then to double the result, which is represented by $x + 1$, multiply by 2: $y = 2(x + 1)$. At first, the two functions appear to be different, but using the distributive property gives $y = 2(x + 1) = 2x + 2$. The functions are actually the same function.

Does the equation $y = \frac{2x-3}{5}$ represent a linear function?

Yes, the equation $y = \frac{2x-3}{5}$ represents a linear function. The equation

$y = mx + b$ defines a linear function, and the given equation can be manipulated to be put in this form:

$$y = \frac{2x - 3}{5}$$
$$y = \frac{2x}{5} - \frac{3}{5}$$
$$y = \frac{2}{5}x - \frac{3}{5}$$

Written in this form, the value of m is $\frac{2}{5}$, which represents the slope of the line. The value of b is $-\frac{3}{5}$, which represents the y-intercept of the line. Any equation that can be transformed into the form $y = mx + b$ represent a linear function. Another common form is

$Ax + By = C$, where A, B, and C are real numbers and $B \neq 0$.

The table shows some data points for a linear function. What is the missing value in the table?

x	y
0	
3	50
5	80

The data in the table represent a linear function. For a linear function, the rate of change is equal to the slope. To find the slope, calculate the change in y divided by the change in x for the two given points from the table:

$$m = \frac{80 - 50}{5 - 3} = \frac{30}{2} = 15$$

The rate of change of the linear function is 15. This means for each increase of 1 in the value of x, the value of y increases by 15. Similarly, each decrease of 1 in the value of x decreases the value of y by 15. The x-value 0 is 3 less than 3, so subtract $3 \cdot 15 = 45$ from 50 to get $y = 5$. This is the missing value in the table.

Sketch a Graph That Is Nonlinear, Increasing, and Passes Through (0, 0).

A graph that is nonlinear will not be a straight line. Also, a graph that is increasing must rise from left to right over its entire domain. For the graph to pass through the point (0, 0), draw a curve that is increasing in the third quadrant and heading toward the origin. Pass through the origin, and continue increasing into the first quadrant. A simple function that has a graph like this is the function $y = x^3$. A sketch of the graph is shown.

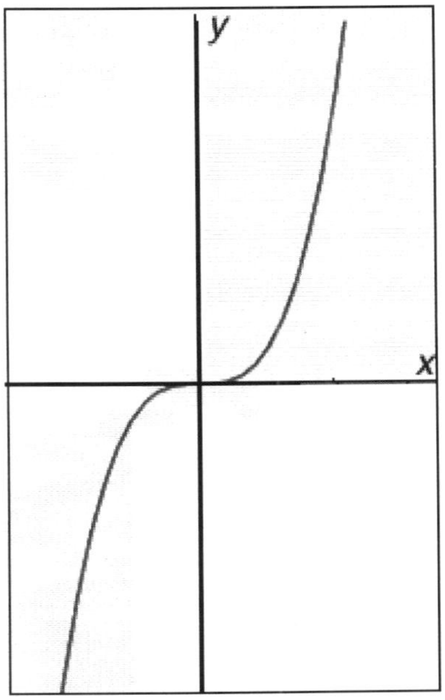

GIVE A SEQUENCE OF TRANSFORMATIONS TO SHOW THAT FIGURE *ABCD* IS CONGRUENT TO FIGURE *MEFG*.

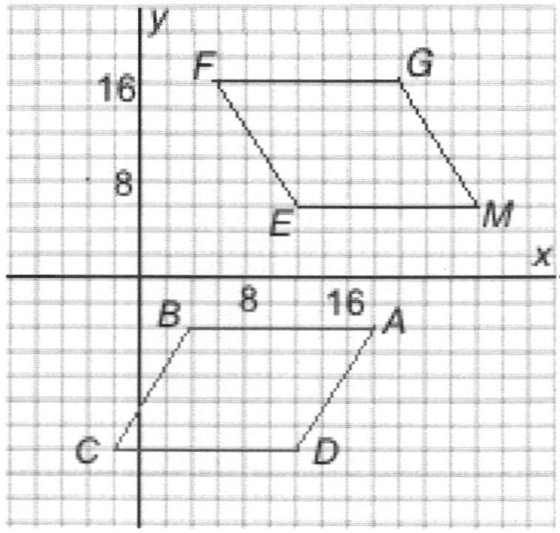

Figure *ABCD* is congruent to figure *MEFG* if there is a sequence of rotations, reflections, or translations that take figure *ABCD* to figure *MEFG*. First, translate figure *ABCD* 8 units to the right and 2 units down. Note that each square on the grid represents 2 units. Then reflect the translated figure over the x-axis, which results in figure *MEFG*. To check the transformations, apply them to the coordinates of the vertices of figure *ABCD*:

- $A(18, -4) \rightarrow (26, -6) \rightarrow (26, 6)$, which is point M
- $B(4, -4) \rightarrow (12, -6) \rightarrow (12, 6)$, which is point E
- $C(-2, -14) \rightarrow (6, -16) \rightarrow (6, 16)$, which is point F
- $D(12, -14) \rightarrow (20, -16) \rightarrow (20, 16)$, which is point G

EFFECT ON THE COORDINATES OF TRIANGLE *GRT* AFTER A REFLECTION OVER THE *X*-AXIS

After a reflection over the x-axis, the y-coordinates of the points of triangle GRT are multiplied by -1. This is because each point on triangle GRT and the corresponding point of the reflection image $G'R'T'$ are the same distance from the x-axis. For example, if point G has coordinates $G(-2, 3)$, then the image G' would have coordinates $G'(-2, -3)$. Even if a vertex is on the x-axis, this will work, because the y-coordinate of the vertex is 0. This means the y-coordinate will remain 0 when multiplied by -1, and the reflection image of the vertex is the same as the original pre-image.

ANY TWO SQUARES ARE SIMILAR

A square is similar to another square if the second can be obtained from the first by a sequence of rotations, reflections, translations, and dilations. Suppose square $ABCD$ in the coordinate plane has vertex $A(x, y)$, and that square $WXYZ$ has vertex $W(m, n)$. Translate square $ABCD$ so that vertex A coincides with vertex W. The translation will be $m - x$ units to the left or right, and $n - y$ units up or down, where the sign of the difference indicates the direction. For example, if $m - x = -3$, translate 3 units left. Then rotate square $ABCD$ about the vertex A until point B is on side WX. Finally, dilate square $ABCD$ by the factor $\frac{WX}{AB}$, with center at vertex A.

THE ANGLE MEASURES OF A TRIANGLE ARE IN THE RATIO 2:3:4. WHAT ARE THE ANGLE MEASURES OF THE TRIANGLE?

Let the smallest angle measure of the triangle be represented by the expression $2x$. Using the ratio 2:3:4, the other two angle measures are given by the expressions $3x$ and $4x$. The sum of the interior angle measures of a triangle is 180°. Write an equation to represent this:

$$\begin{aligned} 2x + 3x + 4x &= 180 \\ 9x &= 180 \\ x &= 20 \end{aligned}$$

To find the angle measures, substitute the value of x for each expression. The angle measures are $2 \cdot 20 = 40°$, $3 \cdot 20 = 60°$, and $4 \cdot 20 = 80°$.

CONVERSE OF A MATHEMATICAL STATEMENT

The converse of a mathematical statement switches the hypotheses of the statement with its conclusion. For example, the Pythagorean Theorem states that if a triangle is a right triangle, then the sum of the squares of the leg lengths is equal to the square of the length of the hypotenuse. The converse states that if the sum of the squares of the leg lengths is equal to the square of the length of the hypotenuse, then the triangle is a right triangle. In this specific instance the converse is true, but in general the converse of a true statement is not necessarily true. For example, if $x = 2$, then $x^2 = 4$. The converse is if $x^2 = 4$, then $x = 2$. This is false, because $x = -2$ or $x = 2$.

A right triangle has side lengths 3 units and $\sqrt{8}$ units. What are the possible lengths of the remaining side?

There are two possibilities for the given side lengths of 3 units and $\sqrt{8}$ units. These could be the lengths of the legs of the right triangle. Or 3 could be the length of the hypotenuse of the right triangle. Note $\sqrt{8}$ cannot be the length of the hypotenuse, because $\sqrt{8} < 3$. Use the Pythagorean Theorem to find the two possible lengths:

$$\begin{aligned} a^2 + b^2 &= c^2 \\ \left(\sqrt{8}\right)^2 + 3^2 &= c^2 \\ c^2 &= 8 + 9 \\ c &= \sqrt{17} \\ a^2 + b^2 &= c^2 \\ \left(\sqrt{8}\right)^2 + b^2 &= 3^2 \\ b^2 &= 9 - 8 \\ b &= 1 \end{aligned}$$

The two possible side lengths are $\sqrt{17}$ units (the missing side length is the hypotenuse) and 1 unit (the missing side length is a leg).

THE DISTANCE FROM (1, A) TO (4, 5) IS 5 UNITS. FIND THE VALUE OF A.

The distance formula states that the distance between two points (x_1, y_1) and (x_2, y_2) is $\sqrt{(x_2 - x_1)^2 + (y_2 - y_1)^2}$. Write an equation using the given points and distance 5 units:

$$\begin{aligned} d &= \sqrt{(x_2 - x_1)^2 + (y_2 - y_1)^2} \\ 5 &= \sqrt{(4 - 1)^2 + (5 - a)^2} \\ 25 &= 9 + (5 - a)^2 \end{aligned}$$

$$16 = (5 - a)^2$$
$$\pm 4 = 5 - a$$
$$a = 1 \; or \; a = 9$$

The distance from (1, 1) to (4, 5) is 5 units, and the distance from (1, 9) to (4, 5) is 5 units

A LARGE PILE OF STONES IS APPROXIMATELY IN THE SHAPE OF A CONE. HOW CAN THE VOLUME OF STONES BE ESTIMATED?

The formula for the volume of a cone is $V = \frac{1}{3}\pi r^2 h$, where r is the radius of the circular base and h is the height. First, estimate the height of the pile by measuring it. If the pile is too tall to measure directly, estimate the leg lengths of a corner of the pile, and then set up a ratio to estimate the height of the pile:

- Measure a and b, a corner of the pile. Measure r, the radius of the pile. Estimate the height h of the pile using the ratio $\frac{a}{b} = \frac{h}{r}$.

The radius r can be measured as half the distance across the base of the pile. Alternatively, if the circumference of the base can be measured, use the equation $C = 2\pi r$ to estimate the value of r.

TIM COLLECTS DATA ON THE TEMPERATURE OVER TWO WEEKS IN THE SUMMER, AND CREATES A SCATTER PLOT. THE INDEPENDENT VARIABLE IS THE NUMBER OF HOURS INTO THE DAY (FOR EXAMPLE, 2 P.M. WOULD BE 14) AND THE DEPENDENT VARIABLE IS THE TEMPERATURE IN °F. WOULD A BEST-FIT LINE LIKELY APPROXIMATE THE DATA WELL?

It is unlikely that a best-fit line will approximate the data well. The reason is that for a best-fit line is used to model a relationship that shows a linear association. In general, temperatures do not steadily increase or decrease from early in the morning to late at night. There is usually a high temperature that occurs sometime in the middle of the day. For this reason, a nonlinear association is more likely to represent the data. This means there is still a relationship between the data, it is just not a linear relationship. It is possible that the scatter plot shows a linear relationship if perhaps the independent variable was only for certain times of the day, such as from 6 a.m. to noon.

THE TABLE SHOWS THE RESULTS FOR A SURVEY ON PREFERRED SCHOOL LUNCHES

	Pizza	**Hot Dog**	**Taco**
Grade 6	85	105	80
Grade 7	95	90	90
Grade 8	120	70	80

To make a relative frequency table, calculate the relative frequencies for each group. Adding the frequencies shows that 85 + 95 + 120 = 300 students prefer pizza, 105 + 90 + 70 = 265 prefer hot dogs, and 80 + 90 + 80 = 250 students prefer tacos. The relative frequencies for the columns, such as pizza, are calculated as follows:

Grade 6 and prefers pizza: $\frac{85}{300} \approx 0.28$
Grade 7 and prefers pizza: $\frac{95}{300} \approx 0.32$
Grade 8 and prefers pizza: $\frac{120}{300} = 0.4$

The other relative frequencies are calculated similarly. The relative frequency table is shown, with the sums of the columns having a sum of 1.

	Pizza	Hot Dog	Taco
Grade 6	0.28	0.40	0.32
Grade 7	0.32	0.34	0.36
Grade 8	0.40	0.26	0.32
Total	1	1	1

Barry says the decimal 0.101001000100001... must be rational, because of the pattern in the digits. What is Barry's error?

A rational number is a number that can be written as a ratio of integers. The decimal representation of a rational number always eventually repeats. This means that the pattern is a finite number of digits that appear over and over again, with no other digits. For example, the decimal 3.852852852... repeats the digits 852 and therefore this number represents a rational number. Also, the decimal 5.61 is rational, because after the 1 there is a pattern of repeating zeros, which typically are not written. The decimal 0.101001000100001... does not, however, have a repeating pattern. The pattern is that the number of zeros between the 1s keeps increasing by 1, but this does not make the decimal a rational number.

Using mental math, estimate the value of the product $(2.48 \times 10^{17})(1.98 \times 10^{23})$

First, estimate the product of 2.48 and 1.98. This can be done first, because the order of the multiplication does not matter. 2.48 is about 2.5, and 1.98 is about 2, so 2.48×1.98 is about $2.5 \times 2 = 5$. Next, multiply the powers of 10. This is a simple application of the multiplication property of exponents, which states that $a^m a^n = a^{m+n}$. So $10^{17} \times 10^{23}$ is equal to 10^{40}. Therefore the product $(2.48 \times 10^{17})(1.98 \times 10^{23})$ is approximately equal to 5×10^{40}.

The solution to $4(x + A) = 2Ax + B$ is *all real numbers*. What are the value of A and B?

To find the values of A and B, first expand the linear equation x:

$$\begin{aligned} 4(x + A) &= 2Ax + B \\ 4x + 4A &= 2Ax + B \end{aligned}$$

When a linear equation has the solution all real numbers, it means that the equation is an identity. In other words, both sides of the equation are the same algebraic expression. The left side of the equation has the term $4x$, and therefore the right hand side must also have this expression:

$$\begin{aligned} 4x &= 2Ax \\ 4 &= 2A \\ A &= 2 \end{aligned}$$

The value of A is 2. This means the left side of the equation is the expression $4x + 8$. Since the constant term is 8, the constant on the right hand side of the equation must be 8. Therefore, $B = 8$. The identity is $4x + 8 = 4x + 8$.

TODAY, TOM IS 8 YEARS OLDER THAN JANET. IN 3 YEARS, TOM WILL BE TWICE AS OLD AS JANET. HOW OLD IS JANET TODAY?

The situation can be represented with a system of linear equations. Let t = Tom's age today and j = Janet's age today. Their ages in 3 years will therefore be $t + 3$ and $j + 3$. Write equations relating their ages today, and their ages in 3 years.

$t = j + 8$ Tom is 8 years older than Janet today.

$t + 3 = 2(j + 3)$ In 3 years, Tom's age $(t + 3)$ is two times Janet's age $(j + 3)$.

Substitute the expression j + 8 for t in the second equation:

$$\begin{aligned} t + 3 &= 2(j + 3) \\ (j + 8) + 3 &= 2(j + 3) \\ j + 11 &= 2j + 6 \\ j &= 5 \end{aligned}$$

Today, Janet is 5 years old.

VERTICAL LINE TEST FOR TESTING WHETHER A RELATION IS A FUNCTION

The vertical line test can be used to test whether a relation is a function, when a graph of the relation is given. For each input of a function, there is exactly one output. Since the inputs are represented on the horizontal axis, any vertical line must pass through the function at most one time. If the vertical line passes through the function twice, then that particular input (on the horizontal axis) would have two distinct corresponding outputs. This would mean the relation does not represent a function. Note that the vertical line test can be used to quickly rule out a relation as a function, but a graph that passes the vertical line test is not necessarily proven to be a function. It would depend on whether the behavior of the entire graph was known for all input values.

DETERMINE HOW THE SLOPE OF A LINEAR GRAPH RELATES TO WHETHER THE GRAPH IS INCREASING, DECREASING, OR NEITHER.

The slope of a linear graph represents the rate of change of the dependent variable per the change in the independent variable. The horizontal axis, on which we measure the independent value (the x value) increases to the right. The vertical axis, on which we measure the dependent value (the y value) increases upwards. Therefore, a graph that increases (goes up) from left to right has a positive slope, and a graph that decreases (goes down) from left to right has a negative slope. If a linear graph is neither increasing nor decreasing, then the rate of change is zero. This means that the slope of the graph is zero, and the graph is a horizontal line.

A SEGMENT WITH ENDPOINTS $A(0, 10)$ AND $B(6, 0)$ IS DILATED BY A FACTOR OF 0.5 WITH THE ORIGIN AS THE CENTER OF DILATION. COMPARE THE LENGTHS OF AB AND $A'B'$.

In order to compare the lengths of AB and $A'B'$, first find the coordinates of points A' and B'. A dilation of 0.5 with the origin as the center of dilation will multiply the coordinates of $A(0, 10)$ and $B(6, 0)$ by 0.5. This gives $A'(0, 5)$ and $B'(3, 0)$. Sketch the segments in the coordinate plane:

Using the Pythagorean Theorem, the length of each segment can be determined:

$AB = \sqrt{6^2 + 10^2} = \sqrt{136} = 2\sqrt{34}$

$A'B' = \sqrt{3^2 + 5^2} = \sqrt{34}$

The length of $A'B'$ is one half the length of AB.

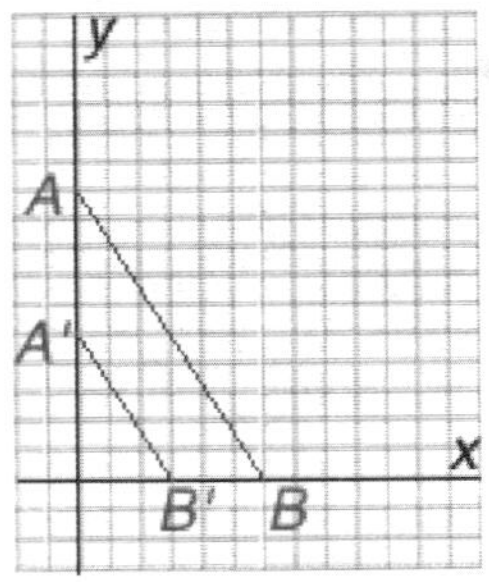

SAM SAYS THAT ANY TWO RIGHT TRIANGLES ARE SIMILAR. USE A SKETCH IN THE COORDINATE PLANE TO DESCRIBE WHY THIS IS NOT TRUE.

Draw two right triangles AOB and AOC in the coordinate plane with right angle O at the origin. The legs of each triangle are drawn on the positive x-axis and positive y-axis, so the triangles both share leg AO. If the triangles are similar, then there must be a dilation that takes triangle AOB to triangle AOC, since the triangles already share right angle O. But any dilation that takes point B to point C must also take point A to point $A' \neq A$, so no such dilation exists.

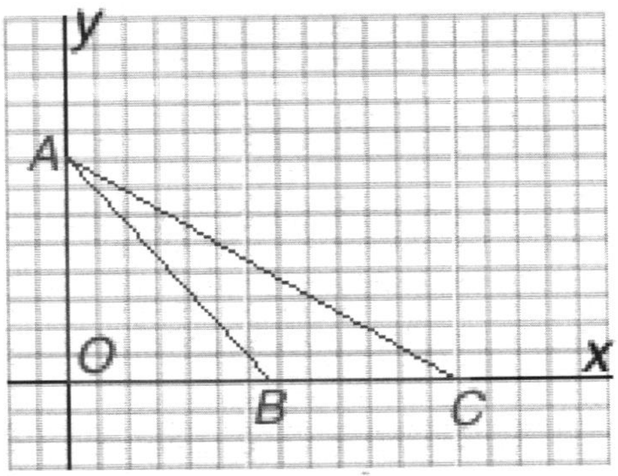

FIND AN EXPRESSION TO REPRESENT THE HEIGHT OF AN EQUILATERAL TRIANGLE WITH SIDE LENGTH S.

Draw an equilateral triangle with side length S. From any vertex, draw the perpendicular to the opposite side. Due to the symmetry of the triangle, it does not matter which vertex is chosen. The length h of the perpendicular segment is the height of the equilateral triangle. Two congruent right triangles are formed, each with a hypotenuse of S (the sides of the original triangle), a leg of length h (the height). and a leg that is half of the side perpendicular to the height, or $0.5S$ in length. Use the Pythagorean Theorem to find an expression for h in terms of S:

$$h^2 + (0.5S)^2 = S^2$$
$$h^2 = S^2 - \frac{S^2}{4}$$
$$h^2 = \frac{3S^2}{4}$$
$$h = \frac{S\sqrt{3}}{2}$$

An expression for the height is $\frac{S\sqrt{3}}{2}$.

FIND AN EXPRESSION THAT GIVES THE DISTANCE FROM (A, B) TO $(-A, -B)$.

The distance between points (a, b) and $(-a, -b)$ can be determined by drawing a sketch and using the Pythagorean Theorem. Draw a vertical and horizontal segment to form a right triangle with a hypotenuse equal to the length of the distance from (a, b) and $(-a, -b)$. The lengths of the legs of the triangle are given by the expressions $2a$ and $2b$. Apply the Pythagorean Theorem:

$$(2b)^2 + (2a)^2 = d^2$$

$$4b^2 + 4a^2 = d^2$$

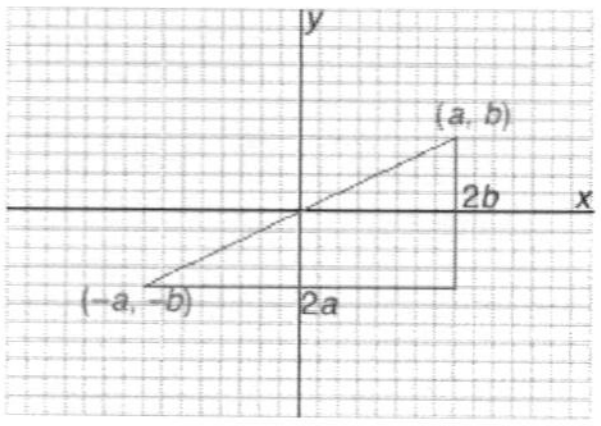

$$d = \sqrt{4(a^2 + b^2)}$$

$$d = 2\sqrt{a^2 + b^2}$$

The distance is $2\sqrt{a^2 + b^2}$ units. This is twice the distance from the origin to the point (a, b).

A CYLINDRICAL MEASURING CUP HAS A CAPACITY OF 2 CUPS. THE CUP HAS A HEIGHT OF 5 INCHES. IF 1 CUP = 14.4375 CUBIC INCHES, DETERMINE THE DIAMETER OF THE CUP TO THE NEAREST TENTH.

Use the formula for the volume of a cylinder, $V = \pi r^2 h$, to determine the radius of the measuring cup:

$V = \pi r^2 h = \pi r^2(5) = 2(14.4375)$

$r^2 = \frac{28.875}{5\pi}$

$r \approx 1.356$

The radius of the cup is about 1.36 inches. The diameter is twice the radius, so the diameter is about 2.7 inches, to the nearest tenth.

DETERMING HOW THE EQUATION OF A LINEAR MODEL CAN HELP PREDICT RESULTS BEYOND THE DATA VALUES

The equation of a linear model represents the best-fit line for the data. This means that a linear relationship is shown in the data, and the equation best gives the value of one categorical variable given the value of the other, particularly for values that fall between the data points. Since a linear equation has a domain of all real numbers, substituting a value of a variable that is beyond the data values will give a corresponding value for the other variable. The further away the value is form the given data, however, the less likely the results will be reliable. This also depends on the actual real-world situation that is being described by the data.

Sum of two rational numbers must be rational by adding and simplifying the sum $\frac{a}{b} + \frac{c}{d}$

A rational number is a ratio of two integers, such as $\frac{2}{3}$. In general, the expressions $\frac{a}{b}$ and $\frac{c}{d}$ represent any two rational numbers, provided that both b and d are not zero. Add the expressions using a common denominator:

$$\frac{a}{b} + \frac{c}{d} = \frac{ad}{db} + \frac{cb}{db} = \frac{ad + cb}{db}$$

The product of two integers results in an integer. Also, the sum of two integers results in an integer. Therefore, the expression $\frac{ad+cb}{db}$ is a ratio of two integers. This means that the sum of any two rational numbers is also rational.

Wendy claims that the irrational number $\sqrt{24}$ is approximately equal to the rational number 12. Find her error.

Wendy most likely made the mistake of thinking a square root of a number is about one half of the number. In general, this is not true. The square root of a number is the number that when squared, or multiplied by itself, gives the original number. To approximate the irrational number $\sqrt{24}$, Wendy should consider perfect squares that are close to 24. The perfect square $25 = 5^2$ is very close to 24, so 5 would be a better approximation for $\sqrt{24}$. Since 24 is a little less than 25, $\sqrt{24}$ is little less than 5. A calculator shows that $4.9^2 = 24.01$.

What is the Reciprocal of the Number -8^{-6}? Use Another Expression with an Integer Exponent.

The reciprocal of a nonzero number a can be written as $\frac{1}{a} = a^{-1}$. Apply this formula to the number -8^{-6}.

$\frac{1}{-8^{-6}} = (-8^{-6})^{-1}$

$= (-1 \cdot 8^{-6})^{-1}$	Rewrite -8^{-6} as $-1 \cdot 8^{-6}$.
$= (-1)^{-1}(8^{-6})^{-1}$	Apply the property $(ab)^n = a^n b^n$.
$= -1 \cdot 8^6$	Apply the property $(a^m)^n = a^{mn}$.
$= -8^6$	Multiply.

The reciprocal of -8^{-6} is -8^6. Note that the reciprocal of a number retains the sign of the number, and that the product of a number and its reciprocal is 1.

How to Cube a Number Written in Scientific Notation

A number is written in scientific notation when it has the form $a \times 10^n$, where $1 \leq a < 10$ and n is an integer. To cube such a number, raise it to the power of 3:

$(a \times 10^n)^3 = (a \times 10^n)(a \times 10^n)(a \times 10^n)$

By the commutative property of multiplication, the factors in the product can be rearranged so that powers of 10 are together:

$(a \times 10^n)(a \times 10^n)(a \times 10^n) = (a \cdot a \cdot a)(10^n \cdot 10^n \cdot 10^n) = a^3 \times 10^{3n}$

This shows that to cube a number of the form $a \times 10^n$, cube the number a and multiply the exponent on the power of 10 by 3. If the number must be written in scientific notation, check that $1 \leq a^3 < 10$.

Characteristics of the Graph of Any Proportional Relationship

A proportional relationship is represented by the equation $y = kx$, where k is a nonzero constant. When $x = 0, y = 0$; therefore, the graph of any proportional relationship is a straight line through the origin. The slope of the line is k. The line cannot be a vertical line, since the equation of a vertical line through the origin is $x = 0$, which is not a proportional relationship and is also not a function. The line also cannot be a horizontal line, because it is assumed the value of k is nonzero.

Josie Solves a One Variable Linear Equation, and Arrives at the Equation 4 = 4. She Concludes the Solution Is $x = 4$. Find Her Mistake.

Josie arrived at an equation that is not dependent on the value of x. This is because the equation 4 = 4 does not have any variables in it. She also arrived at a true statement, which means no matter what value the variable x takes on, the equation will be true. This means that the complete solution to the equation is *all real numbers*. There are therefore an infinite number of solutions to the equation. Had Josie arrived at a false equation, such as 3 = 4, then the equation would have no solution.

Clearing Out Decimals to Get Integer Coefficients When Solving a One Variable Linear Equation

To clear out decimals to get integer coefficients when solving a one variable linear equation, multiply both sides of the equation by the appropriate power of 10. The power is determined by counting the greatest number of digits after the decimal point for all of the coefficients. For example, in the equation $2.4x - 3.2 = 1.5x$, multiply by 10 to get the coefficients 24, 32, and 15. If the equation was $0.24x - 3.2 = 1.5x$, multiply by 100 to get the coefficients 24, 320, and 150. This procedure can help solve an equation with decimal coefficients by eliminating having to add and subtract decimal coefficients of like terms.

What Is the Solution of the System $x + y = 3$ and $2y + 2x = 6$?

Solving the first equation for x gives $y = 3 - x$. Substitute this expression into the 2nd equation:

$$\begin{aligned} 2y + 2x &= 6 \\ 2(3 - x) + 2x &= 6 \\ 6 - 2x + 2x &= 6 \\ 6 &= 6 \end{aligned}$$

The solution leads to a true equation that is independent of the variables. This means that there are infinitely many solutions. The two original equations are actually the same; multiplying the first equation by 2 results in the 2nd equation. Therefore any point (x, y) such that $x + y = 3$ is a solution to the system.

Using a System to Determine if the Sum of Two Numbers Equal the Difference of the Two Numbers

Let both the sum and difference of the two numbers be N. If the two numbers are x and y, write the system as follows:

$$\begin{aligned} x + y &= N \\ x - y &= N \end{aligned}$$

Adding these equations together results in the equation $2x = 2N$, so $x = N$. Substituting $x = N$ into either of the equations gives $y = 0$. This means that for two numbers to have the same sum and difference, one of the numbers must be equal to that sum or difference, and the other number is equal to zero. The solution could be written as an ordered pair as $(N, 0)$, as long as the difference is calculated as $x - y$ and not $y - x$.

What Is the Slope and Y-Intercept of the Graph Represented by the Linear Equation $-3y + 4 = 5x$?

The slope and y-intercept of the graph represented by the linear equation $-3y + 4 = 5x$ can most easily be found by rewriting the equation in the form $y = mx + b$. When written in this slope-intercept form, m is the slope and b is the y-intercept. Solve the equation for y:

$$\begin{aligned} -3y + 4 &= 5x \\ -3y &= 5x - 4 \\ y &= -\frac{5}{3}x + \frac{4}{3} \end{aligned}$$

The slope of the graph is $-\frac{5}{3}$ and the y-intercept is $\frac{4}{3}$. Note that the coefficient of x in a linear equation is the slope only when the equation is solved for y. Similarly, the constant term is the y-intercept only when the equation is solved for y.

A Coupon Entitles the Bearer to 15% off the Price of Lunch. Construct a Function to Give the New Price P of Lunch Given the Original Price X.

The new price of lunch is 15% less than the original price. To find 15% of a number, multiply by 0.15. Since x represents the original price of lunch, the expression 0.15x represents 15% of the original price. The word "off" implies subtraction, that is the 15% discount is subtracted from the original price x. Therefore the new price is $x - 0.15x = 0.85x$. The function p = 0.85x gives the new price p based on the original price x. The 0.85 represents 85%, which is the percent of the original price that is being paid.

Describe Two Different Transformations That Take the Vertex $F(3, -1)$ of Rectangle $FGHJ$ to $F'(1, 3)$.

There are rotations, translations, and reflections that could take vertex $F(3, -1)$ of rectangle $FGHJ$ to $F'(1, 3)$. To determine the translation, subtract coordinates: $1 - 3 = -2$ and $3 - (-1) = 4$, so translating the square 2 units left and 4 units up works. Also, a sketch of the points shows that a rotation of 90° counterclockwise about the origin of vertex $F(3, -1)$ results in the image $F'(1, 3)$. This can be verified by checking the segment from the origin to F is perpendicular to the segment from the origin to F'.

Triangle *ABC* is isosceles. The exterior angle at vertex *B* has a measure of 88°. Find the measures of the angles of the triangle.

Triangle *ABC* is isosceles, which means that two sides are congruent. It also means that the two base angles have the same measure. The exterior angle measure at vertex *B* is 88°, so the measure of angle *B* is 180° – 88° = 92°. If angle B were one of the base angles, then the sum of the base angles would be 92° + 92° = 184°. This is impossible, since the sum of the angle measures of a triangle is 180°. The measures of the base angles have a sum of 88°, so each has a measure of 44°. The angle measures are 44°, 44°, and 92°.

Solving how the diameter of a sphere can be determined given its volume

The formula for the volume of a sphere is $V = \frac{4}{3}\pi r^3$, where *r* is the radius of the sphere. If the volume is known, then the value can be substituted into the formula. Then the equation can be solved for *r* as follows:

$$
\begin{aligned}
V &= \frac{4}{3}\pi r^3 \\
3V &= 4\,\pi r^3 \\
\frac{3V}{4\pi} &= r^3 \\
r &= \sqrt[3]{\frac{3V}{4\pi}}
\end{aligned}
$$

A calculator can be used to get an approximate value of *r* if needed. Finally, the diameter of the sphere is twice the radius, so multiply this value by 2 to get the diameter of the sphere.

Practice Test #1

Practice Questions

1. If $\frac{5}{8}$ is converted into a decimal, how many decimal places will it contain?

a. 2
b. 3
c. 5
d. 4

2. Draw a dot on the number line that corresponds to $\sqrt{7}$?.

3. If a cube has a volume of 27 cubic inches, what is the length of one edge of the cube?

a. $x = -9$
b. $x = 9$
c. $x = -3$
d. $x = 3$

4. A square has a perimeter of approximately 5.66 cm. Which of the following represents the area?

a. 2 cm^2
b. 2.8 cm^2
c. 9.5 cm^2
d. 32 cm^2

5. **Use the grid below to draw a graph that represents the equation $y = 4x$?**

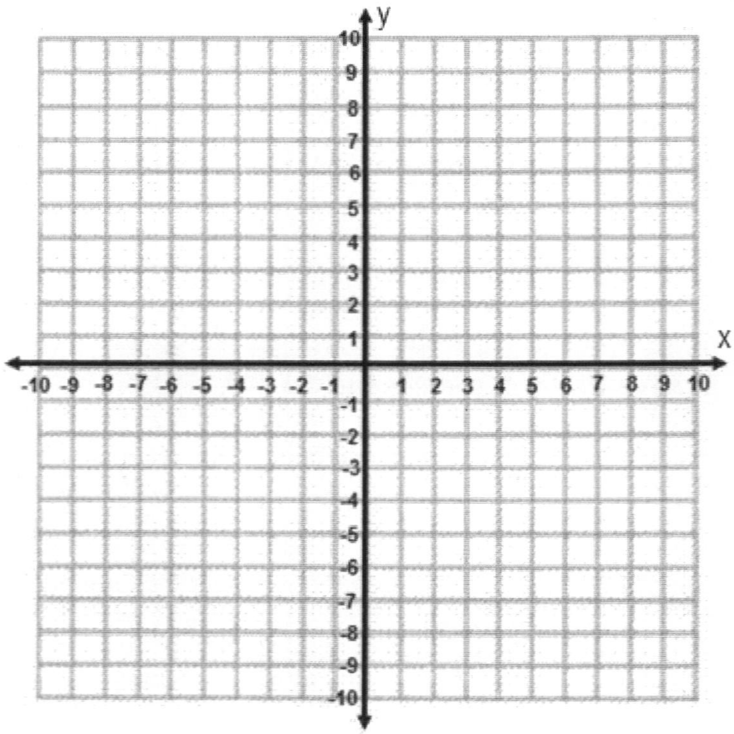

6. **Jonas walks at half the pace of his jogging speed. Draw a graph that shows how far he has gone after *x* minutes.**

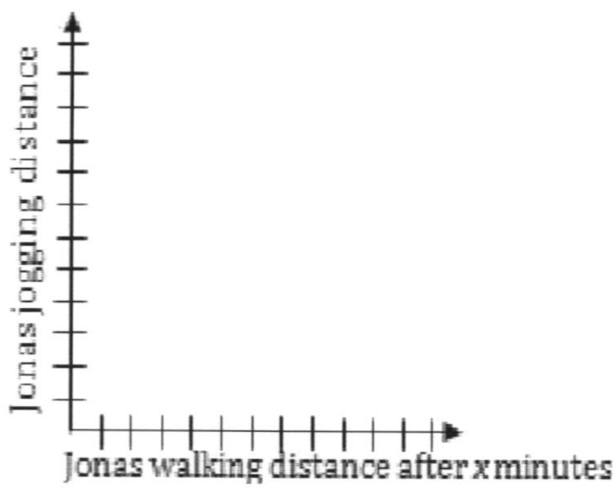

7. **Given the following line, write an equation in slope intercept form.**

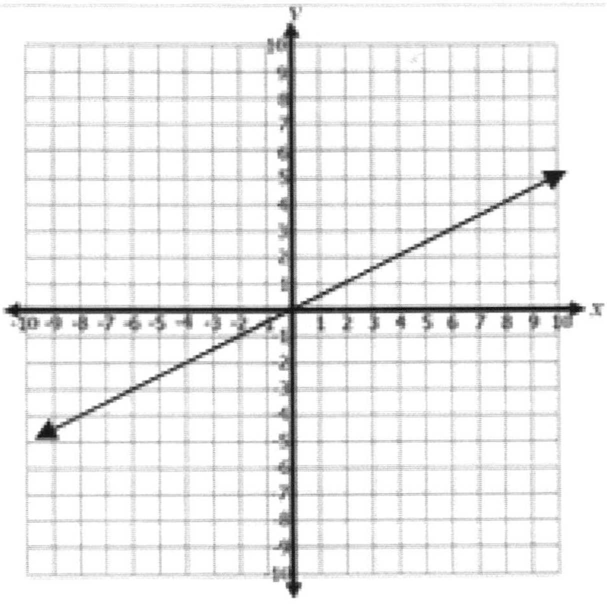

____

8. **Graph the function that is represented by the table below.**

x	y
-2	-1
0	3
1	5
3	9

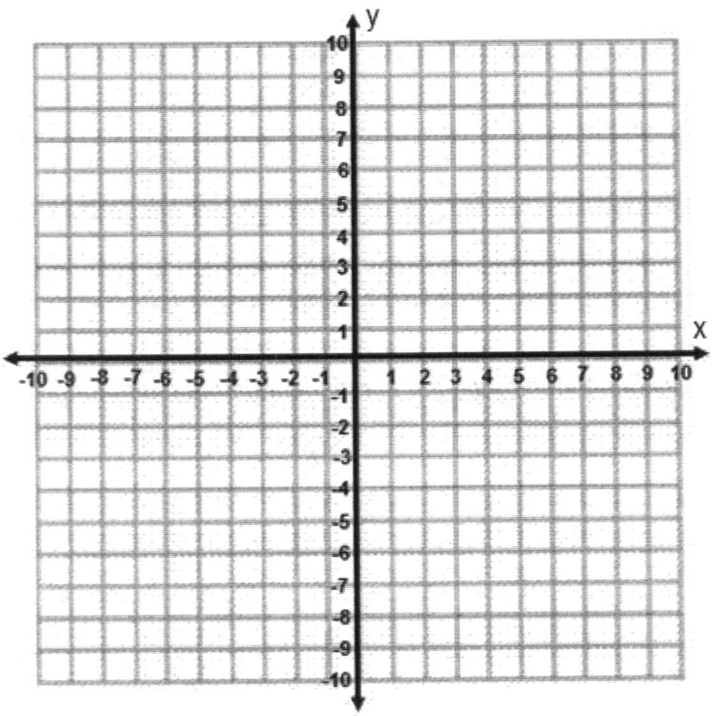

9. Which of the following equations have infinitely many solutions?

a. $3(2x - 5) = 6x - 15$
b. $4x - 8 = 12$
c. $5 = 10x - 15$
d. $7x = 2x + 35$

10. Solve the equation for x: $3(x - 1) = 2(3x - 9)$

a. $x = 2$
b. $x = \frac{8}{3}$
c. $x = -5$
d. $x = 5$

11. Which of the following tables represents a proportional relationship?

a.

x	y
1	-3
2	2
3	7
4	12
5	17
6	22

b.

x	y
1	5
2	8
3	11
4	14
5	17
6	20

c.

x	y
1	6
2	12
3	18
4	24
5	30
6	36

d.

x	y
1	3
2	9
3	15
4	21
5	27
6	33

12. John was given the following equation and asked to solve for x. $\frac{2}{3}x - 1 = 5$. His solution is shown below. Circle the step where he made a mistake and then choose the answer choice that fixes it.

$$\frac{2}{3}x - 1 = 5$$
$$\frac{2}{3}x = 4$$
$$x = \frac{4}{\left(\frac{2}{3}\right)}$$
$$x = 6$$

a. $\frac{2}{3}x = 8$
b. $\frac{2}{3}x = 6$
c. $x = 8$
d. $x = \frac{2}{\left(\frac{2}{3}\right)}$

13. Graph a system of two linear equations that has a single solution at (1, 4).

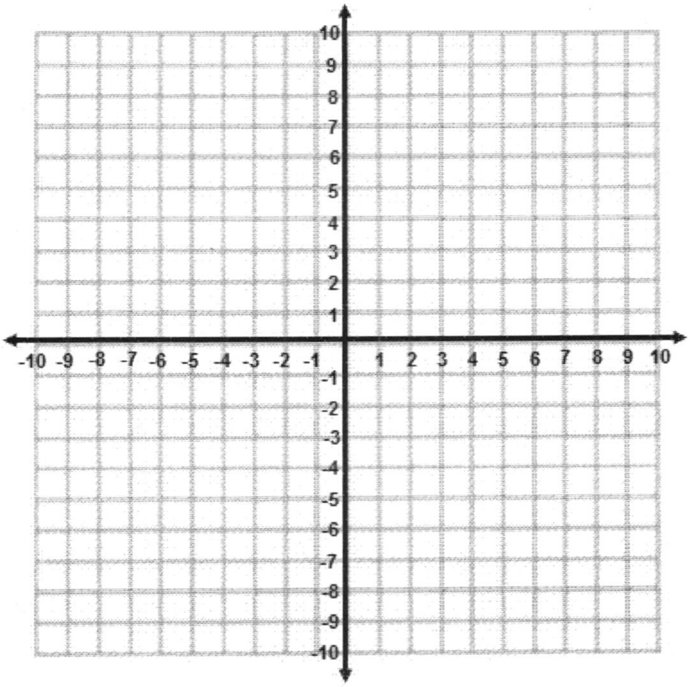

14. Which point represents the solution to the system of linear equations graphed below?

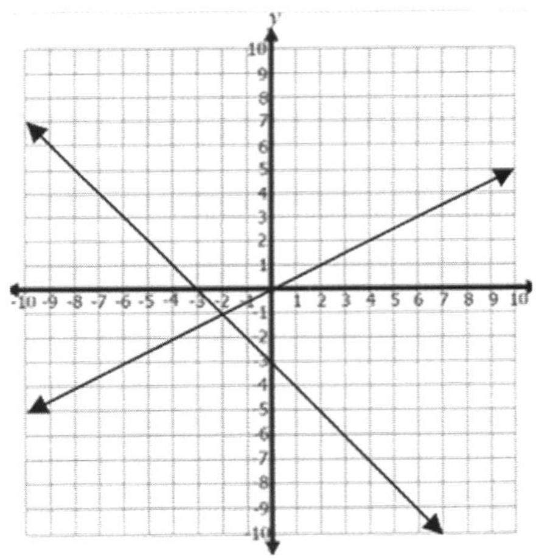

a. $(0, 0)$
b. $(0, -3)$
c. $(-2, -1)$
d. $(-3, 0)$

15. Solve the system of linear equations. $\begin{cases} 3x - 2y = -10 \\ y = 2x + 5 \end{cases}$

a. $(0, 5)$
b. $(-2, 1)$
c. $(1, 2)$
d. $(-3, -4)$

16. Solve the system of linear equations. $\begin{cases} 5x - y = -41 \\ 3x + y = -15 \end{cases}$

a. $(1, -18)$
b. $(-6, 3)$
c. $(-8, 1)$
d. $(-7, 6)$

17. The sum of two numbers is 12. Kelly says the difference of these two numbers must be more than 3. Give an example that supports her claim, and an example that shows her claim is false.

Supports Kelly's claim

□ − □ = □

Shows Kelly's claim is false

□ − □ = □

18. The sum of two numbers is 6. The second number is three more than twice the first number. What are the two numbers?

a. 0 and 6
b. 3 and 3
c. 2 and 4
d. 1 and 5

19. What is the y-intercept of the line $y = 4x - 6$?

a. -4
b. 4
c. 6
d. -6

20. Which function has the higher maximum output?

Function I

x	y
2	3
4	10
5	3

Function II

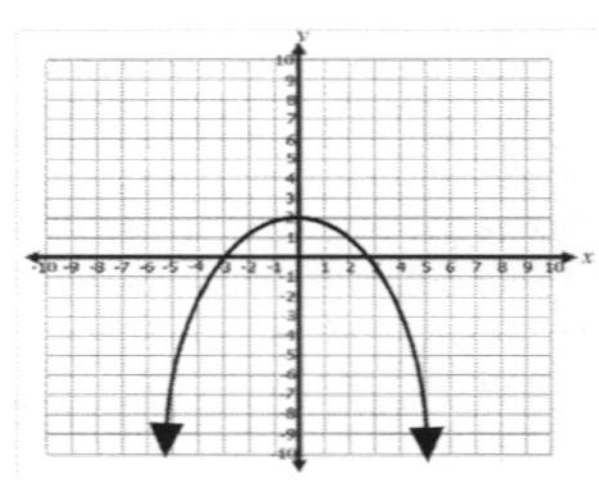

a. Function I
b. Function II
c. They have the same maximum output.
d. Cannot be determined

21. Which function has the greater rate of change?

Function I

x	y
2	4
3	6
4	8

Function II

$y = 5x - 1$

a. Function I
b. Function II
c. They have the same rate of change.
d. Cannot be determined

22. Using the triangle below, which equation would be used to solve for the missing side?

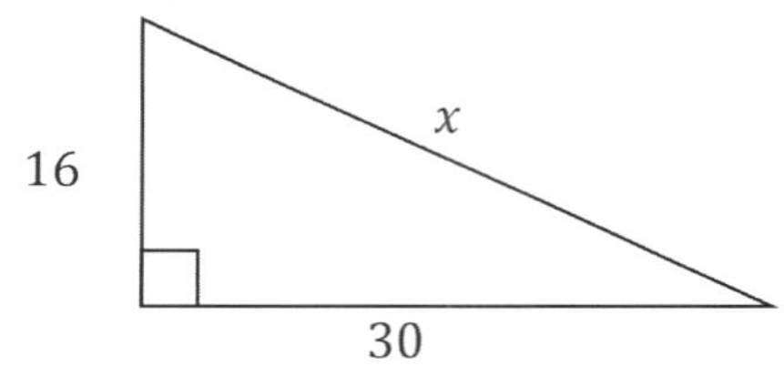

a. $x = \sqrt{16^2 + 30^2}$
b. $x = \sqrt{30^2 - 16^2}$
c. $16 = \sqrt{30^2 - x^2}$
d. $16 = \sqrt{30^2 + x^2}$

23. Which linear function represents the values in the table?

x	0	1	2	3
y	3	1	−1	−3

a. $y = -2x + 1$
b. $y = 2x + 3$
c. $y = 3x + 1$
d. $y = -2x + 3$

24. Look at the graph below. Which equation represents a function with a greater slope?

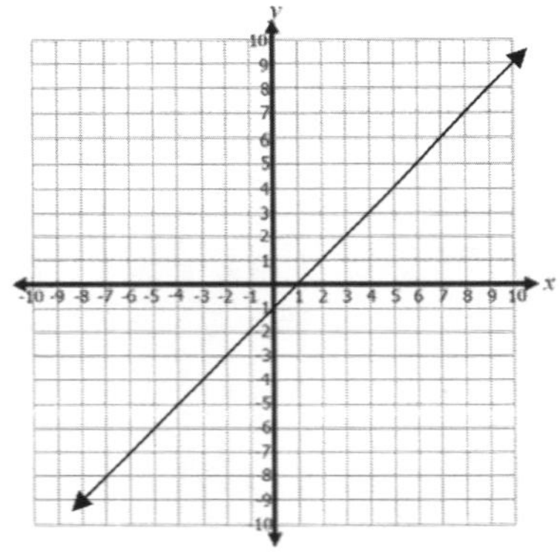

a. $y = x - 2$
b. $y = 2x - 2$
c. $y = \frac{1}{2}x - 1$
d. $y = x - 4$

25. A computer repair shop advertises a discount of 15% off all computer repairs. The original cost to repair Robert's computer is $328. How much money will he save, with the discount?

a. $39.36
b. $42.64
c. $45.92
d. $49.20

26. Which graph best represents the situation?

You leave your house and go to school, you spend the day there, then return home.

a

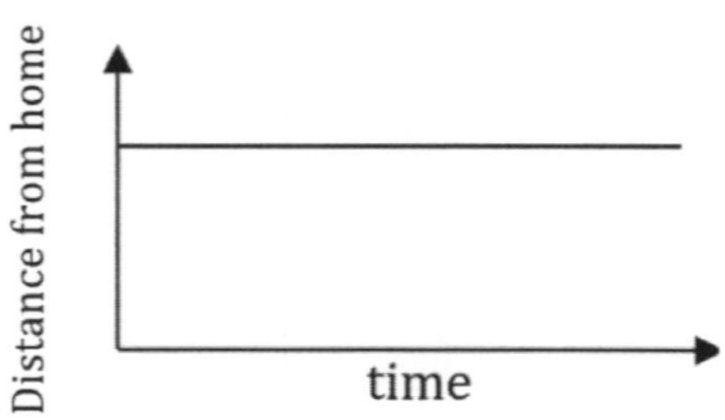

b

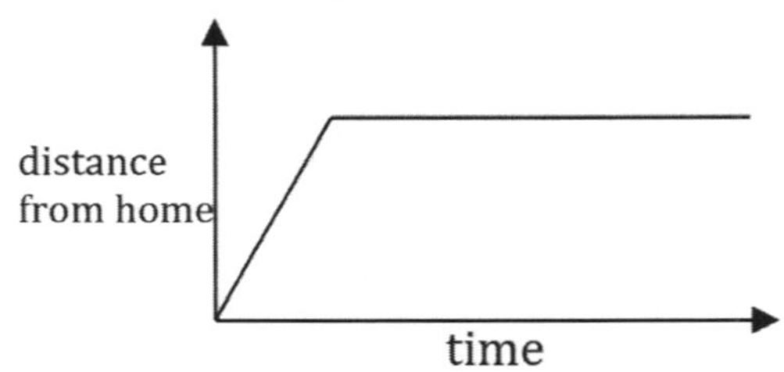

c

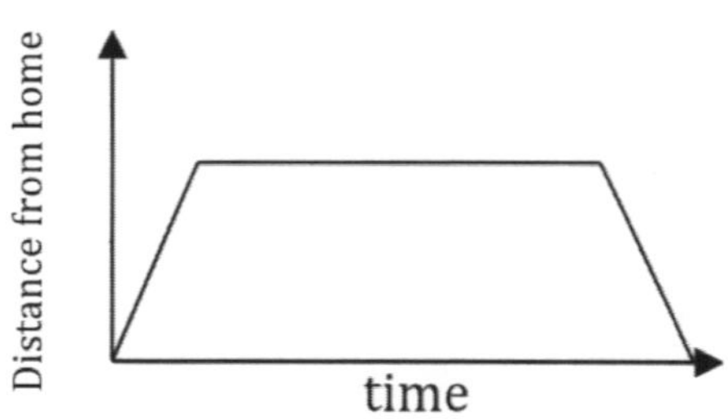

d

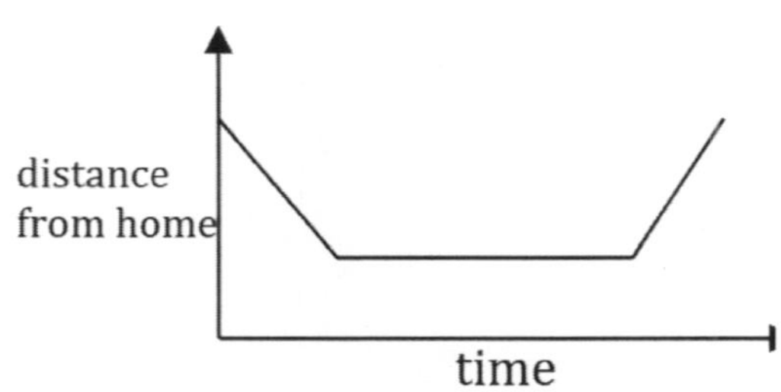

27. Which preimage and image represent a reflection?

a.

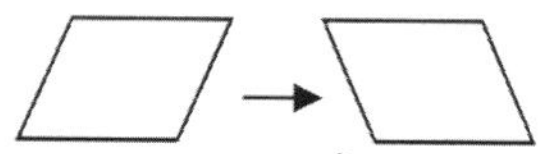

b.

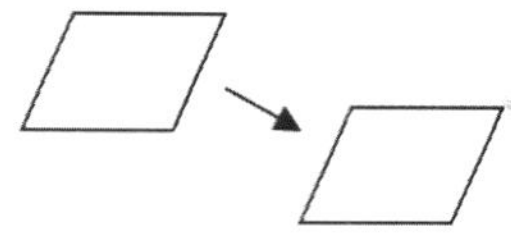

c.

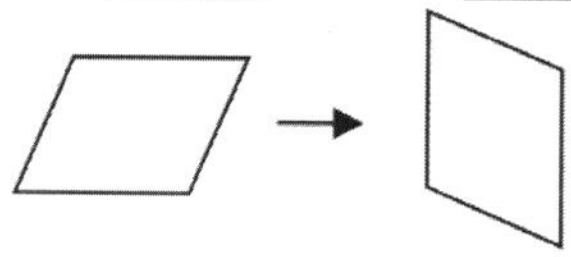

d.

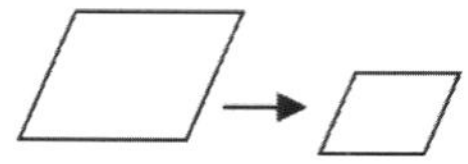

28. Given the image below, what transformation did it undergo?

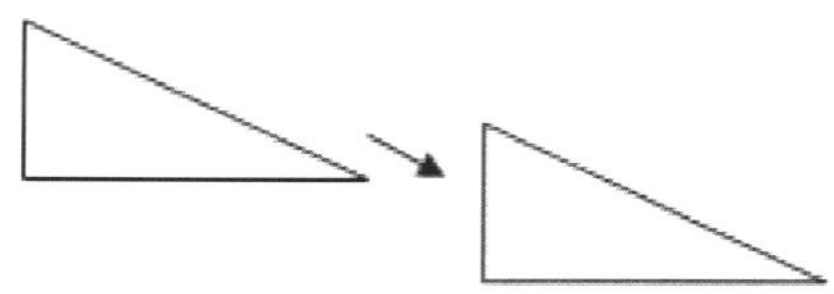

a. Translation
b. Dilation
c. Reflection
d. Rotation

Use the figure below to answer questions 29 and 30.

29. If ΔABC translated 4 units left, what ordered pair would point A map onto?

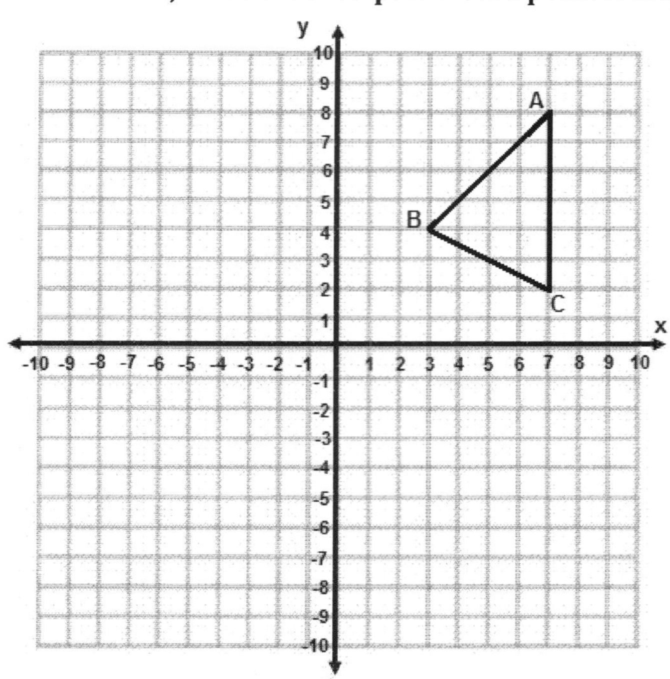

(_____,_____)

30. If ΔABC is reflected across the x-axis what ordered pair would point C map onto?

a. $(-7, 2)$
b. $(2, 7)$
c. $(7, -2)$
d. $(-2, 7)$

31. Gitta consumes approximately 56 grams of protein every 4 days. If she continues to consume the same amount of protein, which of the following represents the number of grams of protein she will consume in 30 days?

a. 360
b. 420
c. 380
d. 400

32. What two transformations will map figure A onto figure B?

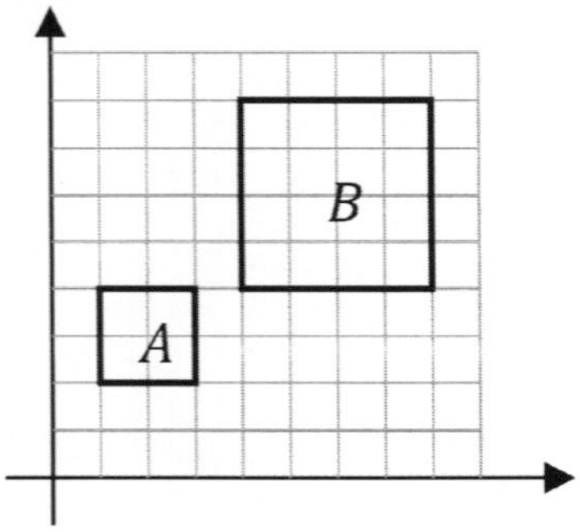

a. Rotation and Translation
b. Translation and Reflection
c. Translation and Dilation
d. Reflection and Rotation

33. Two sides of a right triangle are $\sqrt{17}$ units and $\sqrt{8}$ units. There are two possible lengths for the third side.

What is the shortest possible length, in units? ________
What is the longest possible length, in units? ________

34. Given the graph below draw a rectangle with a perimeter of 30 units. The length of the side of each square is a unit.

35. How many cubic feet of grain will fill the silo if the silo is completely full?

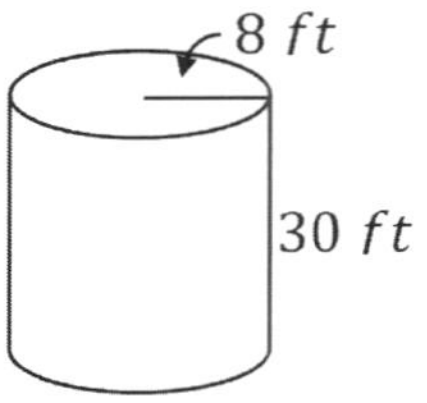

a. 753.6 ft^3
b. 6028.8 ft^3
c. 1920 ft^3
d. $22608 \, ft^3$

36. What kind of association does the scatter plot show?

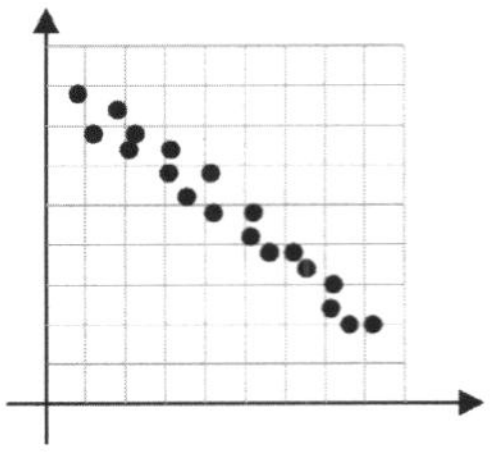

a. Positive, Linear Association
b. Negative, Linear Association
c. Non-linear Association
d. No association can be determined

37. Using the data below, what information was gathered correctly?

Favorite type of music		Age of student surveyed			
	Pop	6-8	9-11	12-14	15-17
	Hip Hop	12	45	50	40
	Country	10	20	45	55
	Other	8	15	20	25
	Pop	8	10	8	20

a. More students prefer country music to pop music.
b. Pop music is preferred to Hip Hop by more students in the 15-17 age category.
c. Hip Hop is preferred to country music by more students in the 9-11 age group.
d. Pop music is preferred to Hip Hop by more students in the 12-14 age group.

38. On the graph below, draw a triangle with a base of 8 units, and a height of 5 units. The length of the side of each square is one unit.

39. David surveyed 10 people to find out whether they owned a car or a truck or both. Using the information below complete the table.

50% owned a car.
30% owned a truck.
10% owned both a car and a truck.

	Car	No Car	Total
Truck			
No Truck			
Total			10

40. Andy has already saved $15. He plans to save $28 per month. Which of the following equations represents the amount of money he will have saved in x months?

a. $y = 15 + 28x$
b. $y = 43x + 15$
c. $y = 43x$
d. $y = 28 + 15x$

41. Which formula is represented by the diagram shown below?

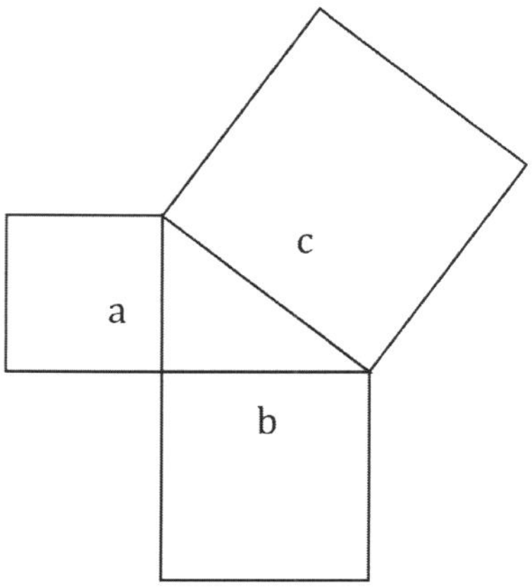

a. $a^2 + b^2 = c^2$
b. $a + b = c$
c. $a + b = c^2$
d. $a^2 + b^2 = c$

42. Bananas cost $.50 per pound. On the graph below, draw a line that shows the proportional relationship between the number of pounds and the cost.

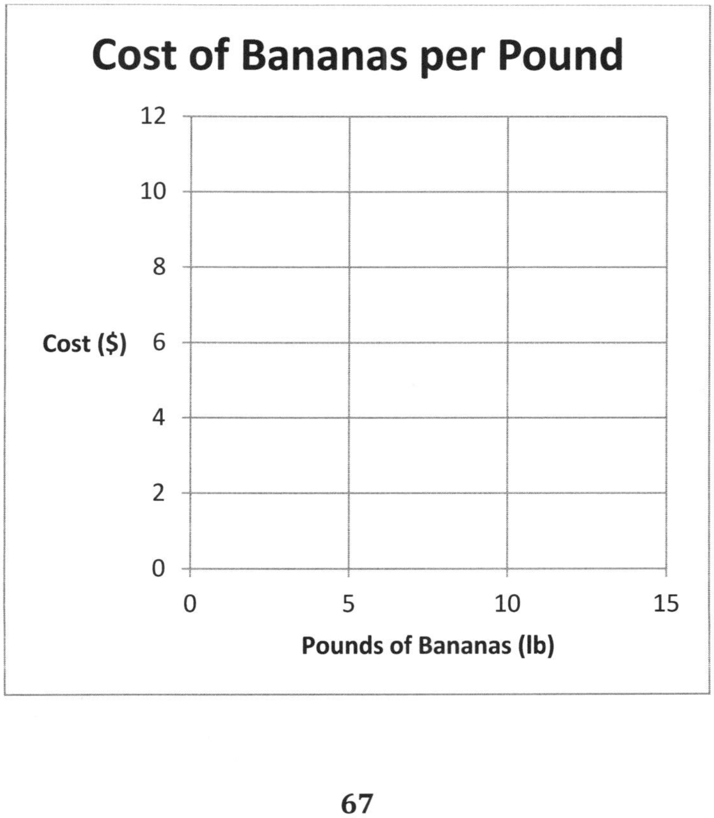

43. A sphere and a cylinder have the same volume. Each figure has a radius of 4 inches. What is the height of the cylinder?

a. $5\frac{1}{2}$
b. $5\frac{1}{3}$
c. $3\frac{1}{5}$
d. $3\frac{1}{2}$

44. Jane is buying oranges. Store A sells oranges 4 for $7, while store B sells oranges 5 for $9. Which store has a better price? Explain you answer.

____

____

____

45. Look at the figure on the graph below. Draw the new image of the figure after the following transformations.

- A reflection across the x-axis
- A horizontal translation 5 units to the left

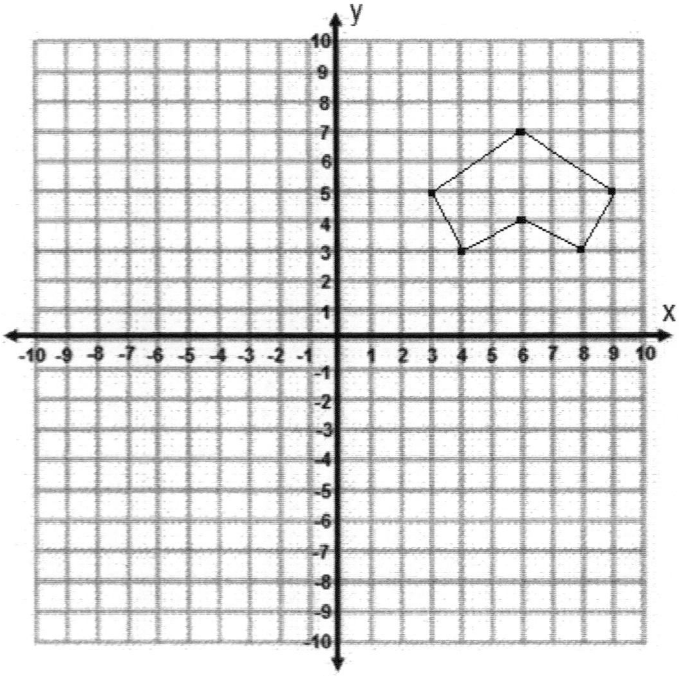

46. Josh and Kate each wrote down a different function. The slope of their functions is the same. Josh's function is $y = 4x - 9$. Give a function that could be Kate's function.

____

47. Decide which of the following numbers is irrational. Choose all that apply.

I. π	IV. .625
II. $\sqrt{16}$	V. $\frac{17}{35}$
III. $\sqrt{8}$	VI. $\sqrt{42}$

48. What is the area of the shaded region in the figure below? The lines cross the very middle of the rectangle. Explain why your answer is correct.

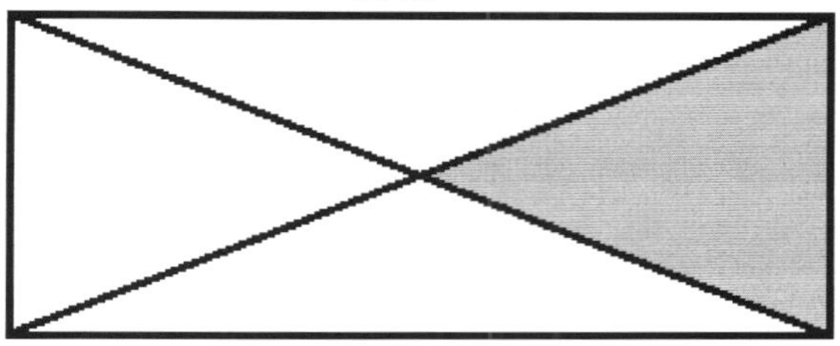

a. 40 sq. in.
b. 20 sq. in.
c. 10 sq. in.
d. 12 sq. in.

____

____

____

49. Which of the following best represents the lateral area of the cylinder shown below?

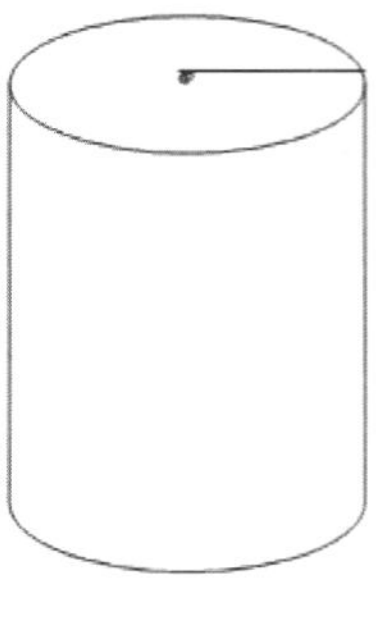

a. 301.4 in^2
b. 75.4 in^2
c. 150.7 in^2
d. 200.8 in^2

50. Part A: A rough sketch of Gabrielle's house is shown below. The image is not to scale. What is the perimeter of the house?

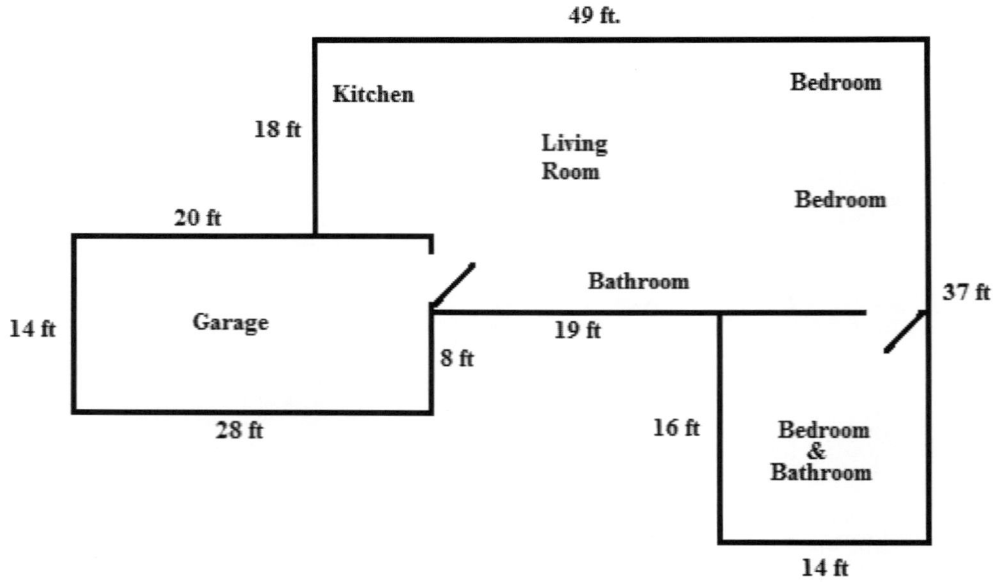

____

Part B: What is the area of the bedroom and bathroom on the bottom right of the drawing?

____

51. Martin wants to buy a new video game. There are 4 different stores that sell the game. Games Inc. sells it for \$54 and they are having a 5% off sale right now. The Video Game Library has it for \$58 and they are having a 10% off sale. Martin also has a coupon for \$2 off a game (applied to the sales price). Gamorama has it for \$51 but has no special deals. Finally, Just for Fun Games has it for \$57 and they are giving \$5 off if you spend \$50 or more. Assuming he wants to buy it as cheap as possible which store should he buy it from?

a. The Video Game Library
b. Games Inc.
c. Just for Fun Games
d. Gamorama

52. Shade $\frac{5}{8}$ on the circle below. Assume all sections are equal.

53. Which of the following equations can be used to find the volume of the cone shown below?

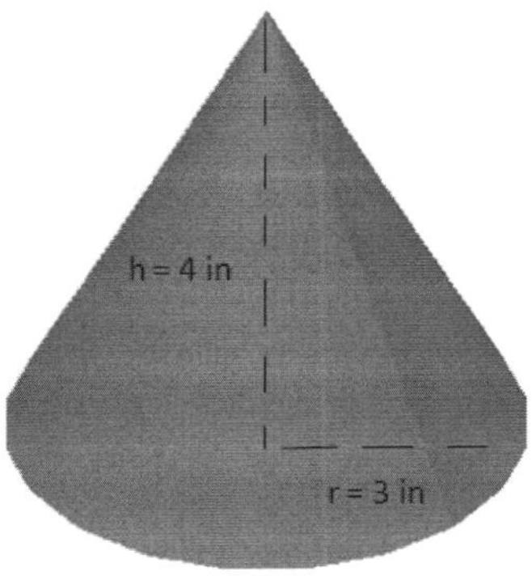

a. $V = \frac{1}{3} \cdot 36\pi \cdot 4$
b. $V = \frac{1}{3} \cdot 3\pi \cdot 4$
c. $V = \frac{1}{3} \cdot 6\pi \cdot 4$
d. $V = \frac{1}{3} \cdot 9\pi \cdot 4$

Answers and Explanations

1. B: $\frac{5}{8}$ as a decimal is .625. That is 3 decimal places.

2. The square root of 7 is approximately 2.64. The dot should be placed like so:

3. D: The volume of a cube is found by cubing the length of one edge of the cube. So given a volume and asked to find the length of the edge of a cube simply take the cube root of the volume.

$$x^3 = 27$$
$$\sqrt[3]{x^3} = \sqrt[3]{27}$$
$$x = 3$$

4. A: Since a square has four equal side lengths, the given perimeter can be divided by 4, in order to determine the length of each side; 5.66 ÷ 4 = 1.415, which is the approximate value of $\sqrt{2}$. Squaring the value of one side gives the area to be approximately 2 cm^2.

5. The equation is in slope-intercept form of $y = mx + b$. In the equation, the slope is 4 and the y-intercept is 0. So the first point is $(0, 0)$ because of the y-intercept, and since the slope is 4, the next point moves 4 spaces up and 1 to the right to the point $(1, 4)$.

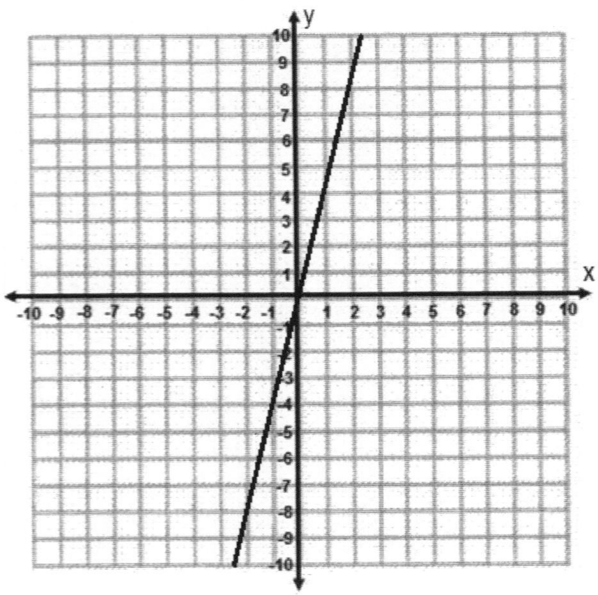

6. If Jonas walks at half the pace he jogs then he will only cover half on the distance when walking. The line is shown below.

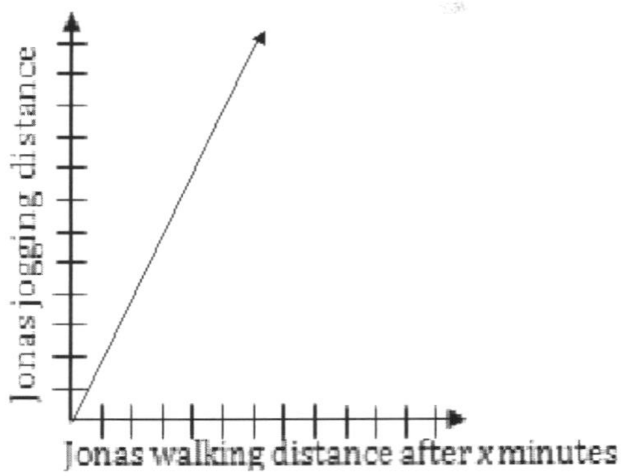

7. To write an equation, first find several points on the graph. For example, (0,0), (2,1), (4,2). To write an equation in slope intercept form first find the y-intercept. This is the point where x=0. Since one of the points we found is (0,0), we know the y-intercept is 0. Next, find slope of the line, which is the change in *y* over the change in *x*. For this example it would be $\frac{2-1}{4-2}$, so the slope is $\frac{1}{2}$. The equation of this line is $y = \frac{1}{2}x$.

8. To graph a line from a table, first plot all of the points on the graph, and the draw a line that connects all of the points.

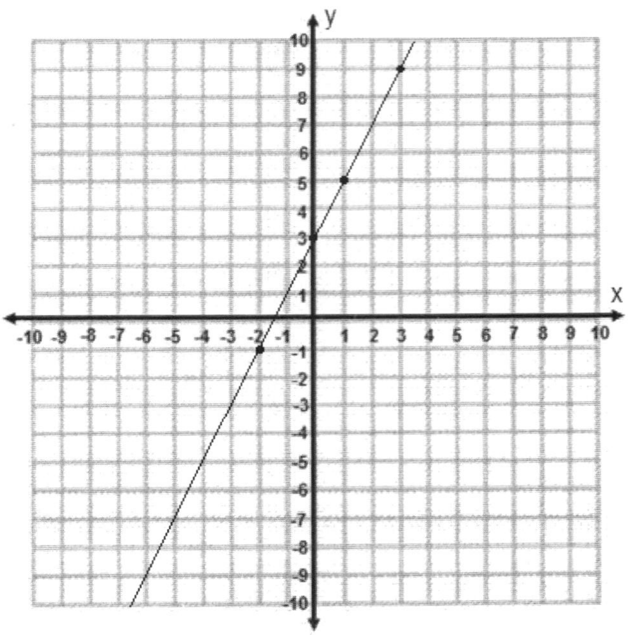

9. A: A is the only one that has infinitely many solutions because when the 3 is distributed across the parentheses, the resulting equation is $6x - 15 = 6x - 15$. Because each side of the equation is identical to the other side, any value of x will make a true statement, so there are infinitely many solutions.

10. D: $3(x-1)=2(3x-9)$

$3x-3=6x-18$	Distribute
$-3=3x-18$	Subtract $3x$ from both sides
$15=3x$	Add 18 to both sides
$5=x$	Divide both sides by 3

11. C: The table for Choice C represents the proportional equation, $y=6x$. A proportion is represented by the equation, $y = kx$, where k represents some constant multiplier. In a proportion the graph of the equation passes through the point, (0, 0), indicating a y-intercept of 0. In other words, the equation does not have a value added to or subtracted from the expression, kx.

12. B. The answer that John gave was:

$$\frac{2}{3}x-1=5$$
$$\frac{2}{3}x=4$$
$$x=\frac{4}{\left(\frac{2}{3}\right)}$$
$$x=6$$

However, he messed up on the second step when he moved the -1 across it should have become a positive 1. That step should be $\frac{2}{3}x=6$.

13. A system of linear equations is a set of linear equations that involve the same set of variables. In this case those variables are x and y. For a system of equations to have only one solution they must only meet once. In this problem the point where they intersect is $(1,4)$. So, any two linear equations that intersect only at the point $(1,4)$ are a solution to this problem. An example is graphed below.

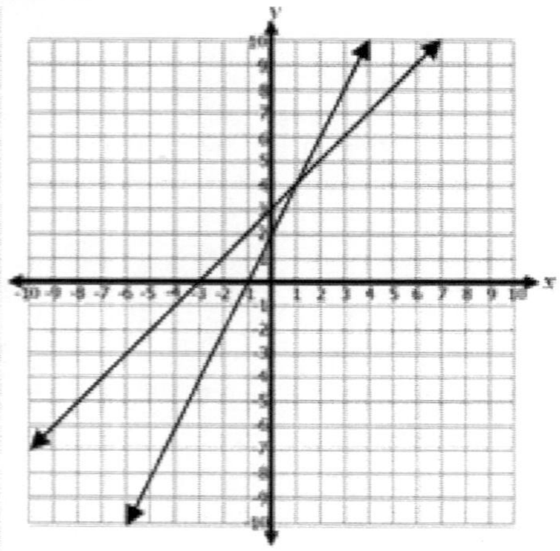

14. C: Given the graph of a system of linear equations, the solution is the point of intersection of the two lines. In this graph, the two lines intersect at $(-2,-1)$.

15. A: $3x-2(2x+5)=-10$ Substitute the expression for y into the other equation

$3x-4x-10=-10$ Distribute the -2 across the parentheses

$-x - 10 = -10$ Combine like terms

$-x = 0$ Add 10 to both sides

$x = 0$ Divide by -1

$y = 2(0) + 5 = 5$ Substitute the value of x into the original equation and simplify.

$(0,5)$ Write your final answer as an ordered pair (x, y)

16. D: $\begin{matrix} 5x - y = -41 \\ 3x + y = -15 \end{matrix}$ the y terms are opposites of each other, use the elimination method.

$8x = -56$ Add the two equations together to get this equation

$x = -7$ Divide both sides by 8

$3(-7) + y = -15$ Substitute the value of x into one of the original equations

$-21 + y = -15$ Multiply

$y = 6$ Add 21 to both sides

$(-7, 6)$ Write your final answer as an ordered pair (x, y)

17. The numbers must add up to equal 12, and one set should have a difference greater than 3 and the other set should have a difference less than 3. An example is given below:

[8] – [4] = [4]

[7] – [5] = [2]

$8 + 4 = 12$, and the difference is greater than 3.

$7 + 5 = 12$, and the difference is less than 3.

18. D: All choices add up to 6, but only the number 5 is three more than twice 1.

Also, the system $\begin{matrix} x + y = 6 \\ y = 2x + 3 \end{matrix}$ can be used to solve the system. The solution is shown below:

$x + (2x + 3) = 6$ Substitute the expression for y into the first equation
$x + 2x + 3 = 6$ Remove parentheses
$3x + 3 = 6$ Combine like terms
$3x = 3$ Subtract 3 from both sides
$x = 1$ Divide by 3 on both sides
$y = 2(1) + 3 = 5$ Substitute value into original equation and simplify
1 and 5

19. D: The line is written in slope-intercept form: $y = mx + b$, and b is the y-intercept. The number that corresponds with b is -6.

20. A: The maximum output in Function I is 10. The maximum output in Function II is 2. Ten is greater than two, so Function I has the higher maximum output.

21. B: The rate of change is also the slope of the linear function, that is, the vertical change over horizontal change. The rate of change for Function I is 2, because the y-value increases 2 for every 1 the input increases. The rate of change for Function II is 5. Function II is written in slope-intercept form and the number that corresponds to the slope is 5. Since 5 is greater than 2, Function II has the greater rate of change.

22. A: The Pythagorean Theorem, $a^2 + b^2 = c^2$, states that the sum of the squares of the legs equals the square of the hypotenuse. Therefore, the hypotenuse is equal to the square root of the sum of the squares of the legs. The legs of the triangle are 16 and 30. The hypotenuse is *x*. The equation solved for the value of the hypotenuse will be $x = \sqrt{16^2 + 30^2}$.

23. D: Based on the table, the rate of change is -2 and the y-intercept is $(0, 3)$. Plugging this information into the slope-intercept form $y = mx + b$, the equation is $y = -2x + 3$.

24. B: The y-intercept of the line is $(0, -1)$. Another point on the line is $(1,0)$. Slope is the vertical change over horizontal change which is $\frac{1}{1} = 1$. The answer choices are already given in slope-intercept form, so you just have to pick the one with a greater slope than 1. The only one that has a greater slope is 2x-2.

25. D: The discount is equal to the product of the original price, \$328, and the percentage of the discount, 0.15; \$328 × 0.15 = \$49.20. Thus, the amount of the discount is equal to \$49.20.

26. C: Since the graphs show the distance from home, and it start at home, the graph begins at the origin. When arriving at school and staying there, the graph is horizontal because the distance from home doesn't change. Then when returning home, the graph returns to the x-axis. Answer C is the only one that shows all three parts.

27. A: Answer A is the only one that represents a reflection or "flip". Answer B represents a translation or "slide". Answer C represents a rotation or turn. Answer D represents a dilation or changing size.

28. A: Answer A is the only one that represents a translation or "slide". Answer B represents a reflection or "flip". Answer C is a dilation. Answer D is a rotation or "turn."

29. Point *A* starts at the ordered pair (7, 8). If it is translated four units left it would end up at the ordered pair (3, 8).

30. C: Point *C* starts at the ordered pair (7, 2). If it is reflected across the x-axis it would end up at the ordered pair (7-2).

31. B: The following proportion can be used to solve the problem: $\frac{56}{4} = \frac{x}{30}$. Solving for *x* gives: $x = 420$. Thus, she consumes 420 grams of protein in 30 days.

32. C: Since the size of B is different from the size of A, a dilation must occur. The only option that has a dilation is C.

33. The Pythagorean Theorem $(a^2 + b^2 = c^2)$ can be used to find the missing side of a right triangle. Given two side measurements the third side can be either the hypotenuse or one of the shorter sides. The shortest possible length for this side can be found by making $\sqrt{17}$ the hypotenuse. The equation would be $(\sqrt{8})^2 + b^2 = (\sqrt{17})^2$. So, $8 + b^2 = 17, b^2 = 9, b = 3$. The shortest the third side could be is 3 units. The equation for the longest possible length would be , $(\sqrt{8})^2 + (\sqrt{17})^2 = c^2$. So, $8 + 17 = c^2, c^2 = 25$, c=5. The longest possible length the third side can be is 5 units.

34. The perimeter of a rectangle is found by adding up the lengths of all of the sides. So, any rectangle that has side lengths that add up to 30 would work. The example below shows a 5 by 6 rectangle.

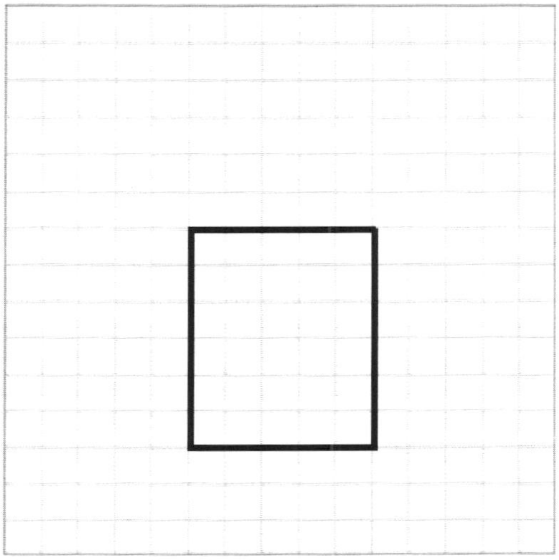

35. B: The formula for the volume of a cylinder is $V = \pi r^2 h$. All values are placed into the formula and simplified. The work is shown below:

$$V = (3.14)(8\,ft)^2(30\,ft)$$
$$V = (3.14)(64\,ft^2)(30\,ft)$$
$$V = 6028.8\,ft^3$$

36. B: A single straight line can be drawn that is close to many of the points. The slope of that line would be negative, so the points have a negative, linear association.

37. C: Answer C is correct because 45 is greater than 20, so Hip Hop is preferred to Country by more students in the age group of 9-11.

38. The triangle below has a base of 8 units and a height of 5 units.

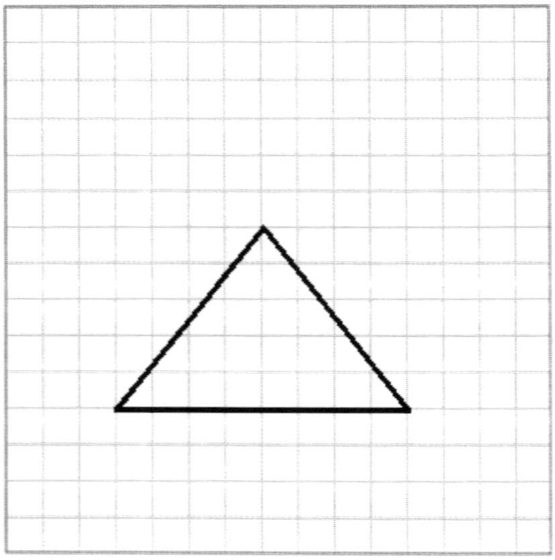

39. Start in the upper leftmost corner. Since 10% own both, that means that 1 person owns both. Then 30% own a truck, so 3 people own a truck but 1 of those owns both. So, only 2 people own just a truck. Then 50% own a car, but one of them owns both, so only 4 own just a car. That leaves 3 people that don't own either one. Add up the columns and rows to get totals and the answer looks like this:

	Car	No Car	Total
Truck	1	2	3
No Truck	4	3	7
Total	5	5	10

40. A: The amount of money he has already saved represents the y-intercept. The amount of money he intends to save per month represents the slope. Thus, his savings can be represented by the equation, $y = 28x + 15$, also written as $y = 15 + 28x$.

41. A: The diagram illustrates the Pythagorean Theorem, or $a^2 + b^2 = c^2$. Notice that squares are attached to each side of the right triangle, revealing the area of one square as a^2, the area of another square as b^2, and the area of the third square as c^2. If the area of the squares equal to a^2 and b^2 are summed, the total area is equal to that of the square equal to c^2.

42. If bananas cost $.50 per pound then for every 2 pounds it would cost $1. The graph that represents this would look like:

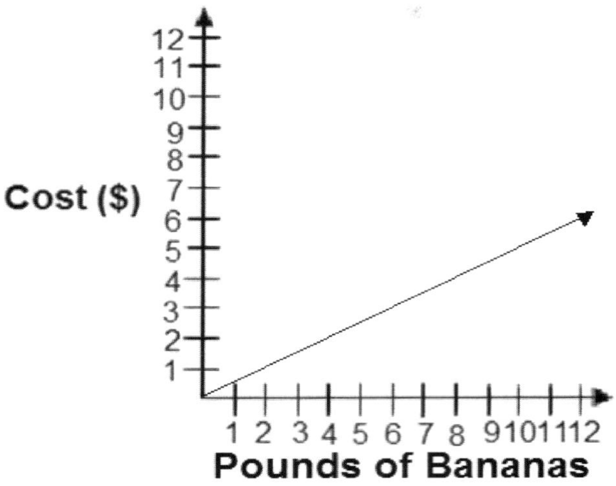

43. B: The volume of a sphere is, $V = \frac{4}{3}\pi r^3$, and the volume of a cylinder is, $V = \pi r^2 h$. Since we know the radius we can solve for the volume of the sphere and we get $V = \frac{4}{3}\pi(4)^3 =$ 268.08257cubic inches. Then, begin to solve for the volume of the cylinder $V = \pi(4)^2 h =$ 268.08257. So, $50.26548h = 268.08257$, and $h = 5\frac{1}{3}$.

44. If Store A sells oranges 4 for $7, then divide 7 by 4 to figure out their cost per orange. 7/4=$1.75 per orange. Store B sells them 5 for $9, so 9/5=$1.80 per orange. This means that Store A has the better price on oranges.

45. A reflection is a transformation where each point on a shape appears at an equal distance on the opposite side of the line of reflection. In this case the line of reflection is the x-axis. After the reflection the image was translated left 5 units. A translation is simply just "sliding" the image. After these two transformations the image would look like this.

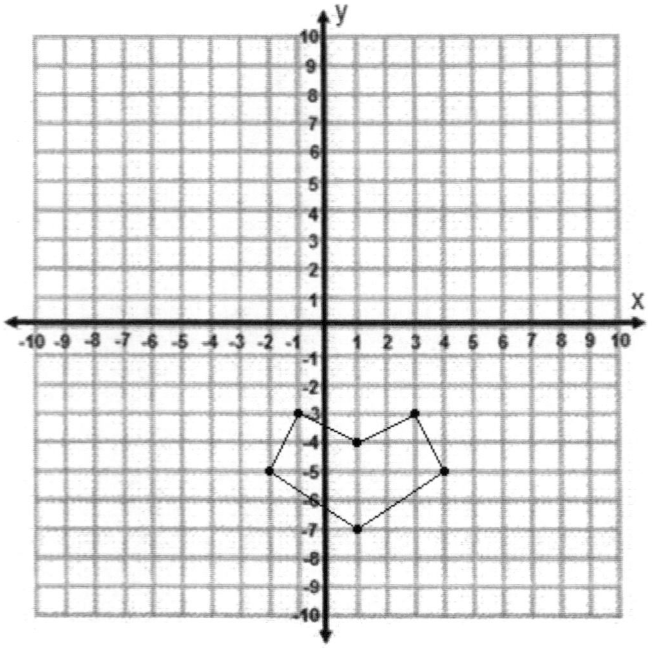

46. Josh's function is $4x - 9$, which means his has a slope of 4. That means Kate's function can be anything with a slope of 4. So for example, hers could be $4x + 2$.

47. I, III, VI: An irrational number is one that cannot be expressed as a simple fraction. There is no fraction that represents π, and $\sqrt{8}$ and the $\sqrt{42}$ also cannot be represented as a fraction.

48. C: The shaded region is a triangle with a base of 4 inches and a height of 5 inches. Since the lines cross in the middle of the rectangle we know that the height of the triangle is half the length of the rectangle or 5 inches. The formula for area of a triangle is $\frac{1}{2}bh$. Where b is the length of the base and h is the height. So, the area of the shaded region is $\frac{1}{2}(4)(5) = 10$ sq. inches.

49. C: The lateral area of a cylinder can be determined by using the formula, $A = 2\pi rh$, where r represents the radius, h represents the height, and A represents the lateral area. Substituting the radius of 4 inches and height of 6 inches gives: $2\pi \cdot 4 \cdot 6$, which equals 48π, or approximately 150.7. Thus, the lateral area of the cylinder is approximately 150.7 square inches.

50. Part A: 223 ft.: The perimeter of a figure is the distance around the outside. To find the perimeter simply add all of the side lengths together. $18 + 20 + 14 + 28 + 8 + 19 + 16 + 14 + 37 + 49 = 223$.

51. A: First figure out the price at each store. Games Inc. has it for $54 but they have a 5% off sale. So, solve for 95% of $54, which is $54(.95)= $51.30. Then the Video Game Library has it for $58 and they have a 10% off sale plus Martin's $2 off coupon. So, solve for 90% of $58 and then subtract $2. The price is $58(.9)= $52.20-$2.00= $50.20. Then Gamorama has it for $51 but has no specials. Finally, Just for Fun Games has it for $57 and is giving $5 off of $50 or more. Which make their price $57-$5= $52. So, Martin can get the best deal at the Video Game Library.

52. The circle is divided into 16ths. So, convert $\frac{5}{8}$ to 16ths to get $\frac{10}{16}$. Then shade 10 slices of the circle as shown below.

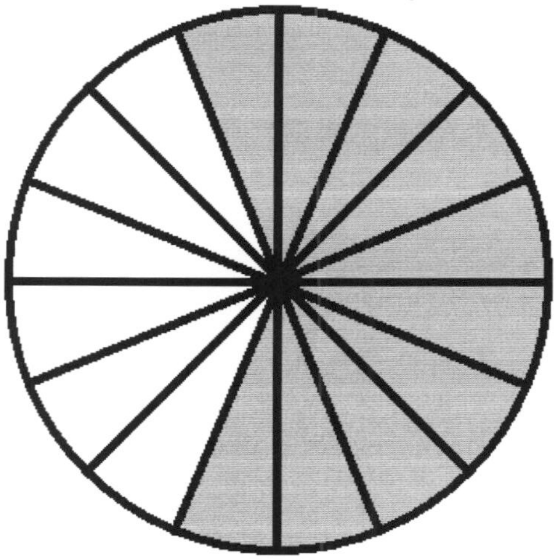

53. D: The volume of a cone can be determined by using the formula, $V = \frac{1}{3}\pi r^2 h$, where r represents the radius and h represents the height. Substitution of the values for the radius and height into the formula gives: $V = \frac{1}{3} \cdot \pi(3)^2 \cdot 4$, which can be rewritten as: $V = \frac{1}{3} \cdot 9\pi \cdot 4$.

Practice Test #2

Practice Questions

1. Which fraction is equivalent to 0.375?

a. $\frac{4}{25}$
b. $\frac{1}{6}$
c. $\frac{3}{8}$
d. $\frac{3}{20}$

2. $2\sqrt{5}$ is between which two numbers?

a. 4 and 5
b. 2 and 3
c. 3 and 4
d. 10 and 11

3. A square has an area of 64 square units. What is the length of one side square?

a. 7
b. 6
c. 10
d. 8

4. The total length of the world's coastlines is about 315,000 miles. Which answer expresses this in scientific notation?

a. 3.15×10^{-6}
b. 3.15×10^{-5}
c. 3.15×10^{6}
d. 3.15×10^{5}

5. Marla is a growing a plant. The plants growth is graphed below. Based on the graph how many feet does the plant grow each week?

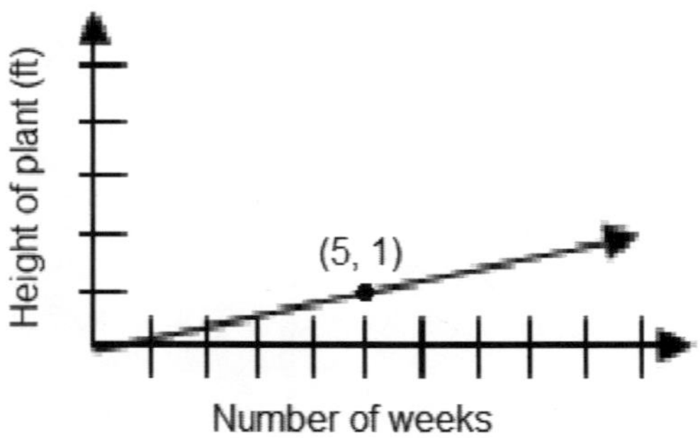

________________feet

6. John's Gym charges its members according to the equation $C = 40m$ where m is the number of months and C represents the total cost to each customer after m months. Ralph's Recreation Room charges its members according to the equation $C = 45m$. What relationship can be determined about the monthly cost to the members of each company?

a. John's monthly membership fee is equal to Ralph's monthly membership fee.
b. John's monthly membership fee is more than Ralph's monthly membership fee.
c. John's monthly membership fee is less than Ralph's monthly membership fee.
d. No relationship between the monthly membership fees can be determined.

7. What relationship can be determined about the slopes of line p and line q?

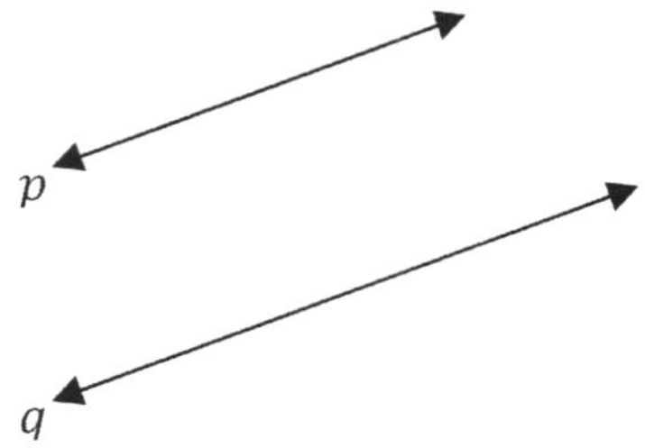

a. The slope of line p is equal to the slope of line q.
b. The slope of line p is greater than the slope of line q.
c. The slope of line p is less than the slope of line q.
d. No relationship can be determined from the graph.

8. A pentagon with side lengths of 9 cm, 18 cm, 24 cm, 18 cm, and 9 cm is dilated by a scale factor of $\frac{1}{3}$. Which of the following represents the dimensions of the dilated pentagon?

a. 3 cm, 9 cm, 8 cm, 9 cm, 3 cm
b. 6 cm, 3 cm, 12 cm, 6 cm, 3 cm
c. 3 cm, 6 cm, 8 cm, 6 cm, 3 cm
d. 6 cm, 18 cm, 9 cm, 6 cm, 9 cm

9. Write an equation for line m in slope-intercept form.

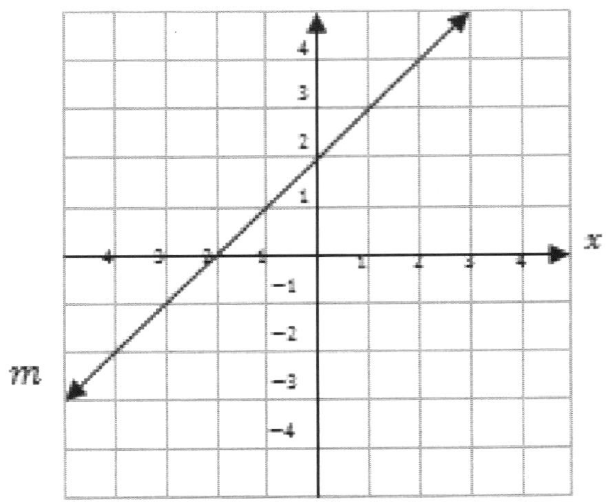

____

10. Given the equation $+1 = \_x + \_$. Create an equation with no solutions, one solution, and infinitely many solutions.

Equation with no solutions

$$6x + 1 = \square x + \square$$

Equation with one solution

$$6x + 1 = \square x + \square$$

Equation with infinitely many solutions

$$6x + 1 = \square x + \square$$

11. How many solutions does the equation $2(7x - 5) = 14x - 8$ have?

a. None
b. One
c. Two
d. Infinitely many solutions

12. Solve the equation for x. $\frac{1}{2}(x - 7) = \frac{3}{5}(5x + 15)$. Explain the steps you took to solve the equation.

a. $x = -\frac{16}{5}$
b. $x = \frac{16}{5}$
c. $x = 5$
d. $x = -5$

____

____

____

13. Which point is a solution to the system $\begin{cases} 2x + y = 7 \\ x - y = 2 \end{cases}$?

a. $(4, -1)$
b. $(2, 3)$
c. $(3, 1)$
d. $(5, 3)$

14. Solve the system of linear equations $\begin{cases} y = -x + 3 \\ y = \frac{1}{2}x + 9 \end{cases}$.

a. $(1, 2)$
b. $(-4,7)$
c. $(4, -1)$
d. $(6, 12)$

15. A fundraising group charges $0.25 per cookie and has a daily expense of $18. Which of the following describes the steps that need to be taken, in order to calculate the daily profit, when selling 49 cookies?

a. Multiply 49 by $0.25 and subtract $18
b. Multiply 49 by $0.25 and divide by $18
c. Multiply 49 by $0.25 and add $18
d. Multiply 49 by $18 and subtract $0.25

16. Mark and Sally were selling candy bars for their school fundraiser. Together they sold 49 candy bars. Sally sold one less than four times the amount Mark sold. How many candy bars did Sally sell?

a. 29
b. 34
c. 39
d. 44

17. A school auditorium has 600 seats total on the main floor and balcony combined. There are 5 times as many seats on the main floor than there are in the balcony. Based on this information fill in the equation below. Explain why your answer is correct.

$$\square + \square = \square$$

Seats on main floor	+	Seats in balcony	=	Total number of seats

____

____

____

18. Which of the following graphs is __not__ a function?

a.
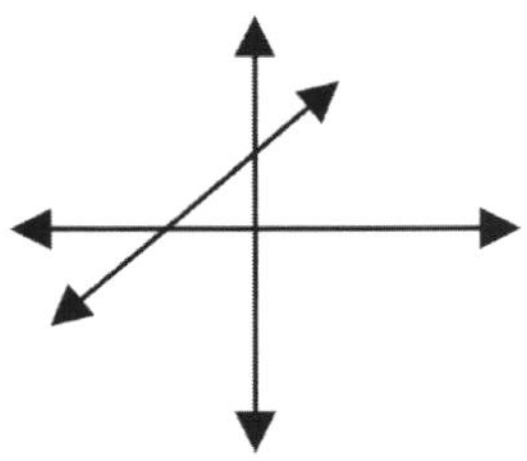

b.
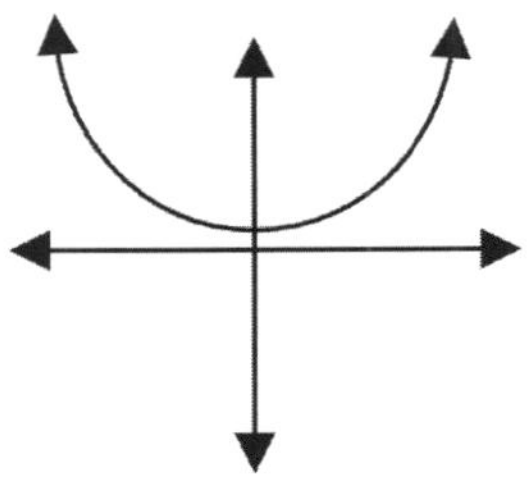

c.
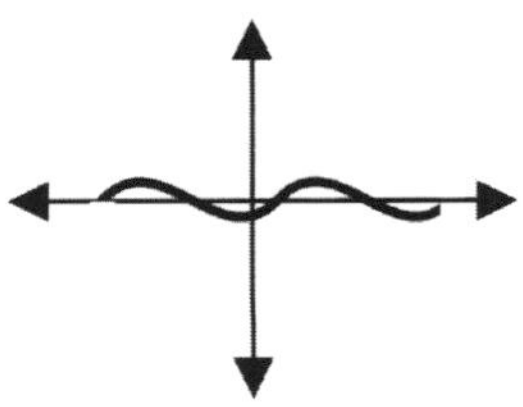

d.
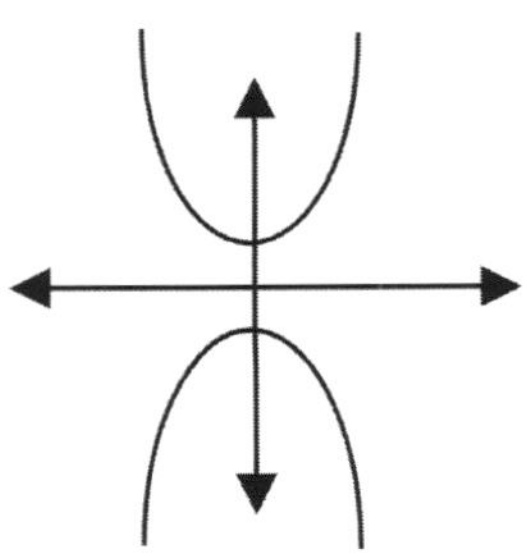

19. Which transformations can be done to image *A* to produce image *B*? Circle all that apply.

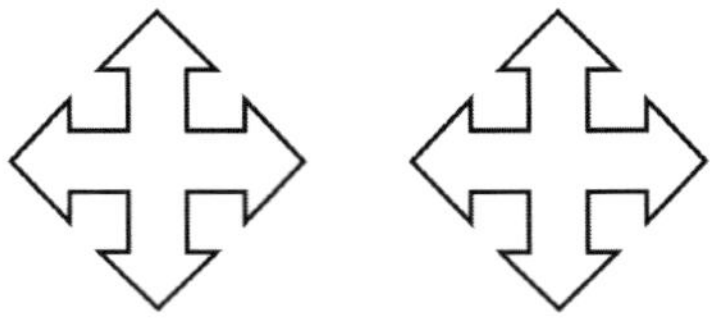

A *B*

Translation
Rotation
Reflection
Dilation

20. Which of the following describes a proportional relationship?

a. Jonathan opens a savings account, with an initial deposit of $150, and deposits $125 per month
b. Bruce pays his employees $12 per hour worked, during the month of December, as well as a $250 bonus
c. Alvin pays $28 per month for his phone service, plus $0.07 for each long distance minute used
d. Kevin drives 65 miles per hour

21. Which function has the smaller range?

Function *I*

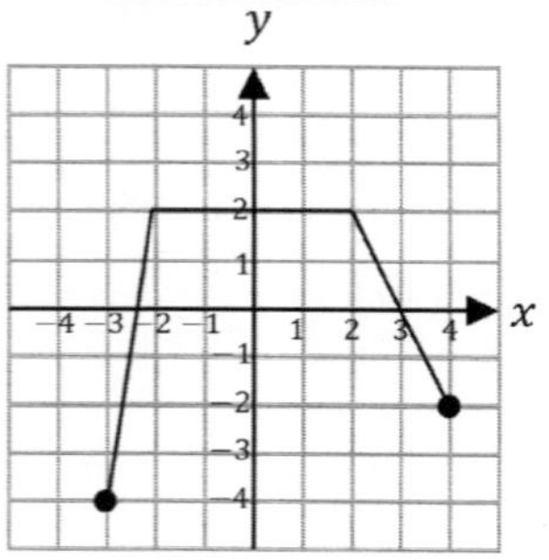

Function *II*

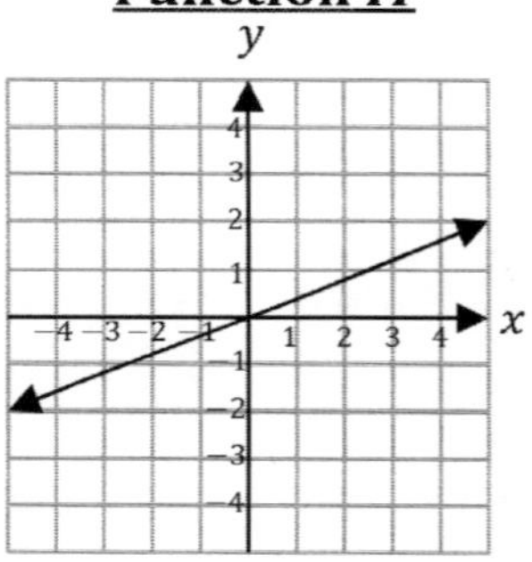

a. Function I
b. Functions II
c. They have the same y-intercept
d. Cannot be determined

22. Which function below is <u>not</u> linear?

a. $4y + 3x = -1$
b. $2x - y = 5$
c. $y = 3x - 9$
d. $y = \sqrt{x} + 2$

23. Write a function in slope-intercept form based on the values in the table?

x	0	2	4	5
y	−2	8	18	23

____

24. Which function represents the graph?

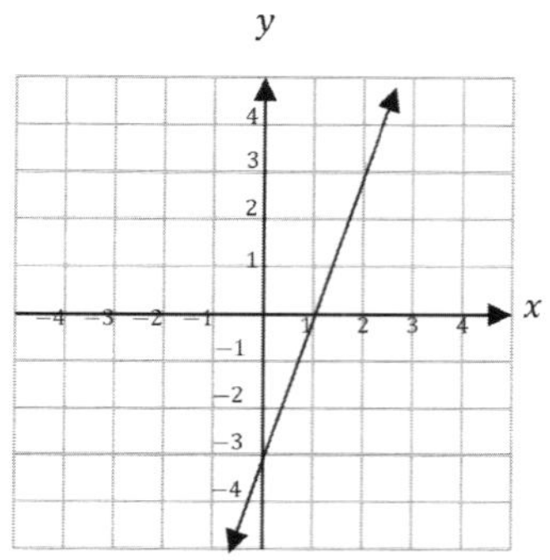

a. $y = 3x + 1$
b. $y = 3x - 3$
c. $y = -3x + 1$
d. $y = -3x - 3$

25. Triangle DEF is similar to Triangle ABC. What is the length of $\overline{DF}$?

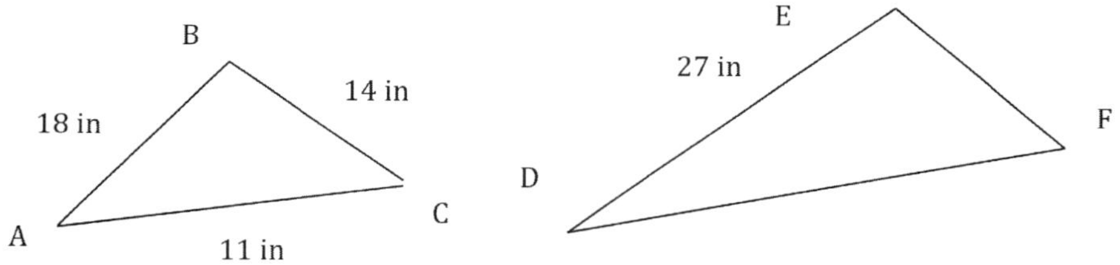

a. 18.5 in
b. 20 in
c. 16.5 in
d. 22 in

26. On which interval is the function decreasing?

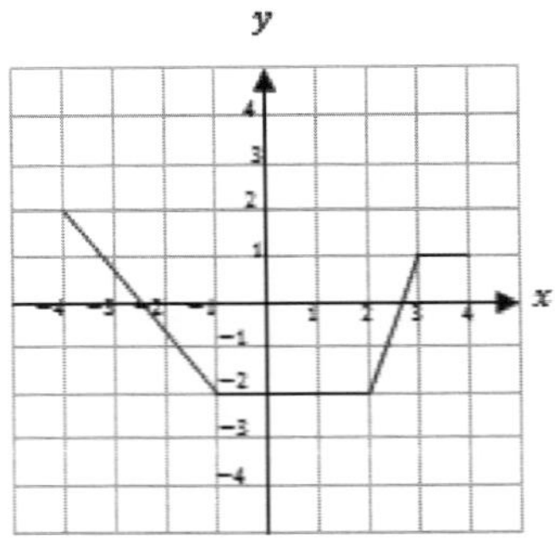

____ < x < ____

27. Which graph best represents the situation?

The speed of your bike as you start rolling down a hill without pedaling, pedal at a constant rate on a level sidewalk, and stop at a store.

a. 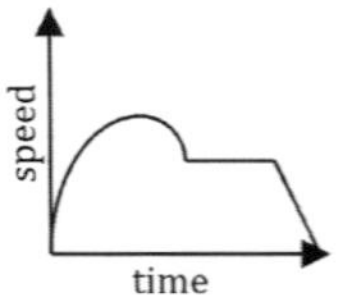

b. 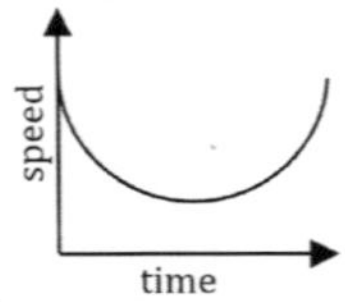

c. 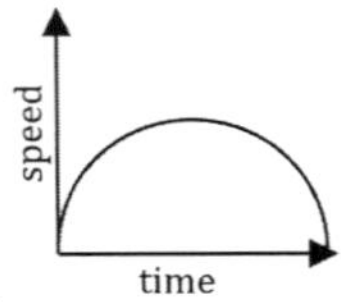

d. 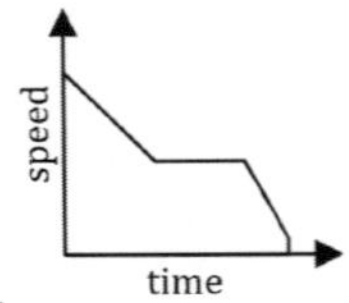

28. Which two shapes represent a rotation?

a. 

b. 

c. 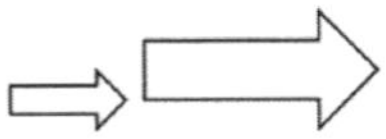

d. 

29. A cylinder has a height of 9 inches and a radius of 4 inches. If the height remains the same, but the radius increases by 8 inches, what is the effect on the volume of the cylinder?

a. It will be 7 times larger
b. It will be 9 times larger
c. It will increase by 3,548 cubic inches
d. It will increase by 3,576 cubic inches

30. What transformation do the two shapes below represent?

31. If ΔABC is dilated by a factor of 3, what is the new measure of $\overline{AB}$?

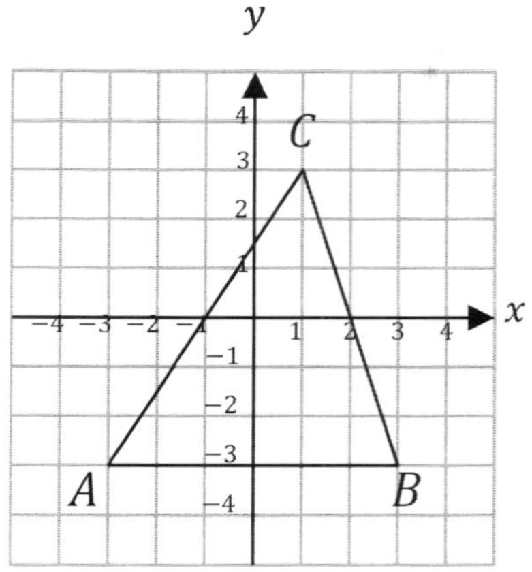

a. 2
b. 6
c. 9
d. 18

32. What two transformations will map figure *A* onto figure *B*?

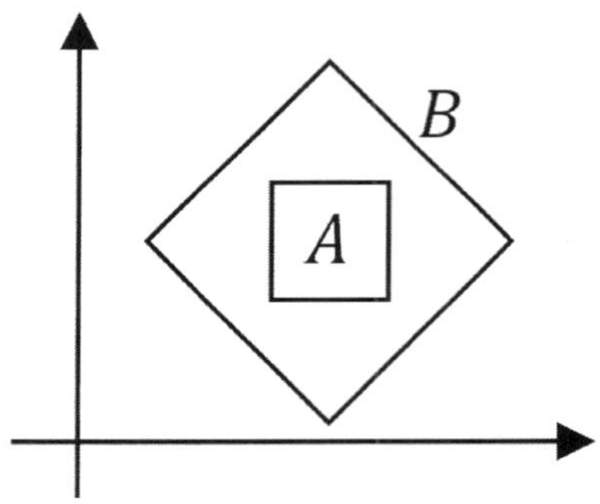

a. Rotation and Translation
b. Reflection and Translation
c. Rotation and Dilation
d. Translation and Dilation

33. Given triangle ΔABC, with the $m\angle C$ is 60°, and the $m\angle B$ is $\frac{2}{3}$ of $m\angle C$. What is the $m\angle A$?

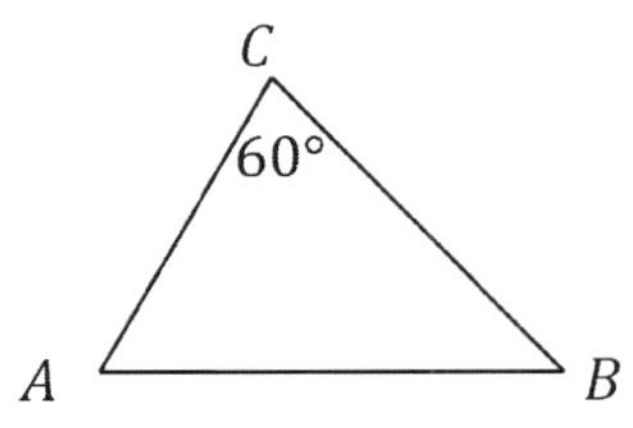

a. 45°
b. 105°
c. 60°
d. 80°

34. How much more is $AB + BC$ than AC?

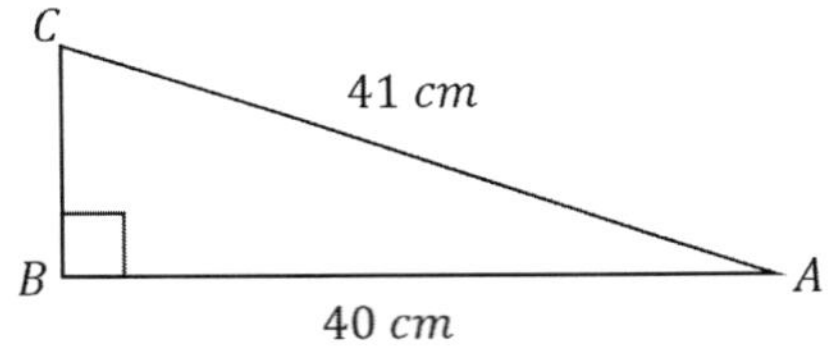

a. 8 cm
b. 9 cm
c. 10 cm
d. 11 cm

35. Given the two points on the graph below, what is the distance between them? Explain the process to find the distance between two points.

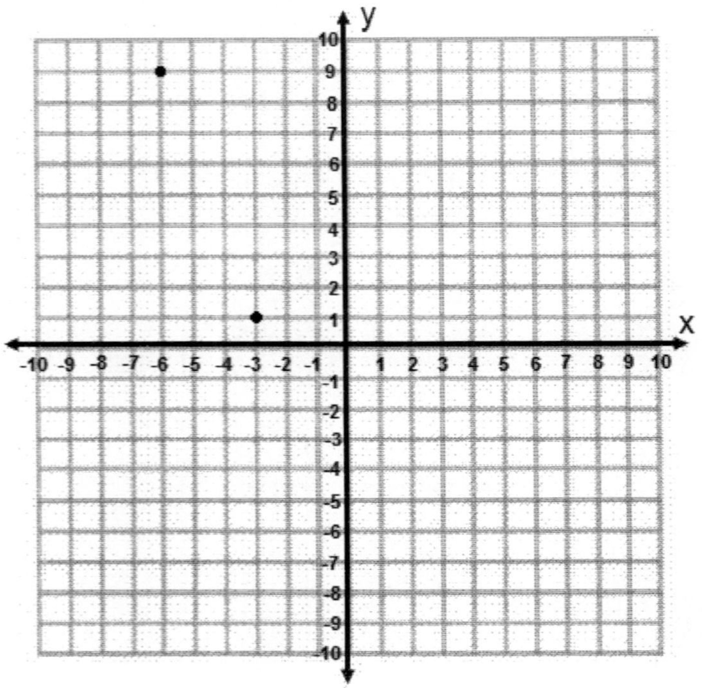

____

____

____

36. Carmen flips a coin and draws a card from a deck. What is the probability she gets heads and draws an ace?

a. $\frac{15}{26}$
b. $\frac{4}{13}$
c. $\frac{1}{26}$
d. $\frac{2}{13}$

37. Label the side lengths of the rectangular prism so that the volume equals 48 cu. in.

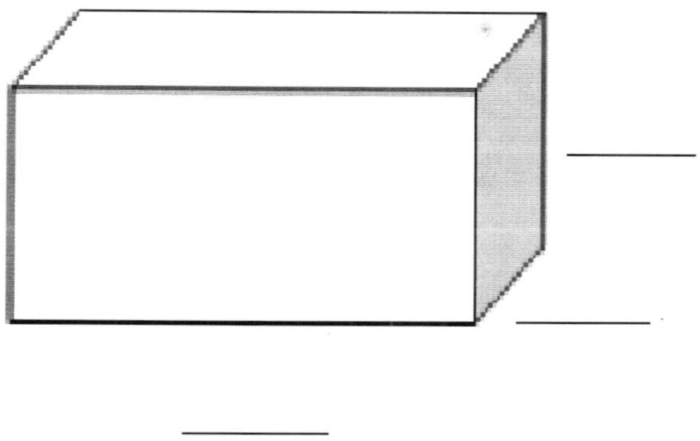

38. Which of the following vertices represents the reflection of the triangle, shown below, about the *x*-axis?

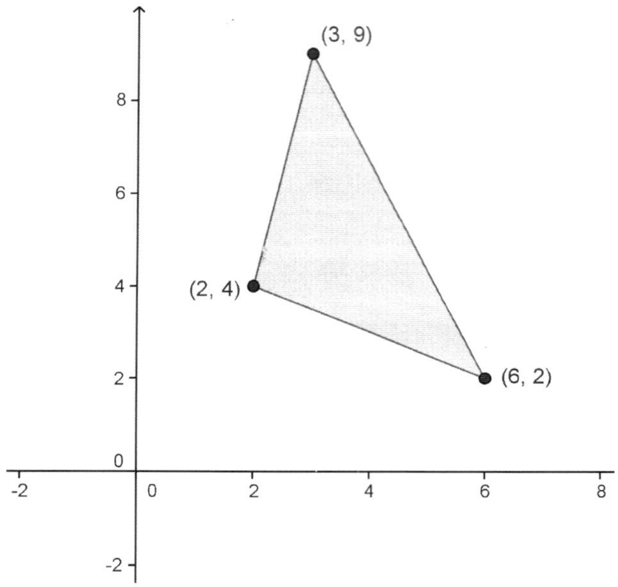

a. (3, −9), (2, −4), (6, −2)
b. (−3, −9), (−2, −4), (−6, −2)
c. (9, 3), (4, 2), (2, 6)
d. (−3, 9), (−2, 4), (−6, 2)

39. What is the volume of the sphere?

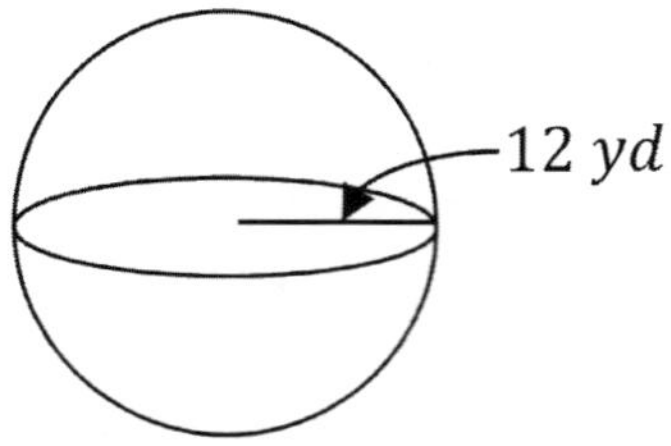

a. 904.32 cubic yard
b. 7234.56 cubic yards
c. 602.88 cubic yards
d. 57876.48 cubic yards

40. Which line best represents the line-of-fit for the data?

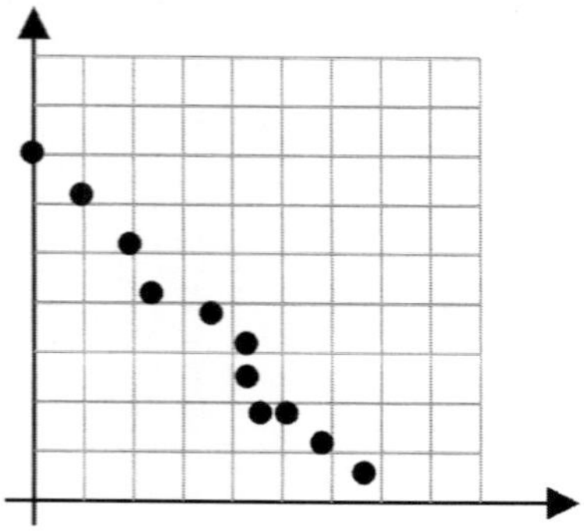

a. $y = -7x + 1$
b. $y = 7x - 1$
c. $y = -x + 7$
d. $y = x - 7$

41. Using the data at the right, what statement best describes the rate of change?

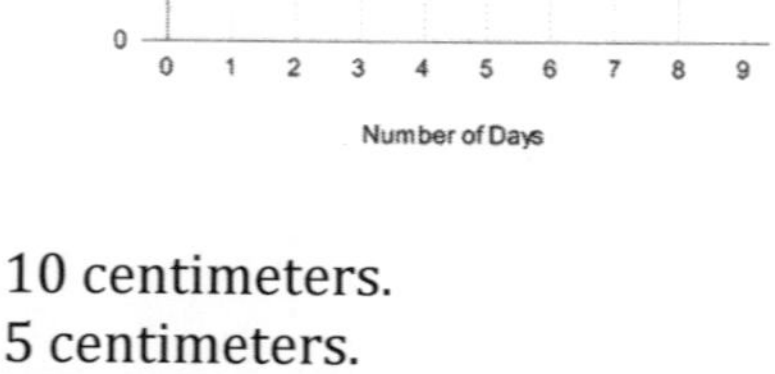

a. Every day, the snow melts 10 centimeters.
b. Every day, the snow melts 5 centimeters.
c. Every day, the snow increases by 10 centimeters.
d. Every day, the snow increases by 5 centimeters.

42. Using the data below, decide if the following statement is true or false.

	Blue Eyes	Not Blue Eyes	Total
Male	15	80	95
Female	20	60	80
Total	35	140	175

A larger percentage of women have blue eyes than the percentage of men who have blue eyes.

____

43. Blake is 3 years younger than Susie. Susie is 4 years younger than twice the age of Brett. Brett is 2 years older than Jaime and Jaime is 9 years old. Place their names on the number line below with an arrow pointing to their age.

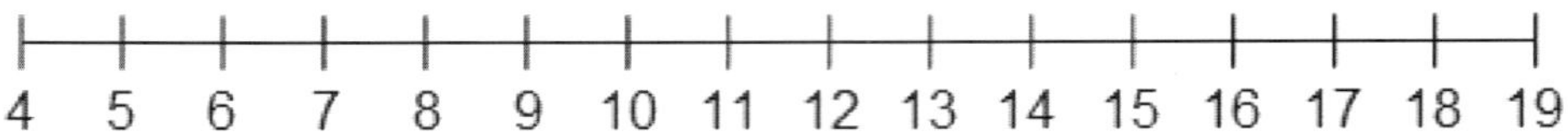

44. Which of the following best represents the lateral surface area of the cylinder shown below?

a. 351.68 in^2
b. 703.36 in^2
c. 904.72 in^2
d. 1,202.96 in^2

45. A game uses a coin and two dice. To win the game a player must have both of the following results:

The coin must land on heads when it is flipped
The total of the dice roll must be ten or greater
What are the odds of a player winning this game?

a. $\frac{3}{8}$
b. $\frac{1}{10}$
c. $\frac{1}{8}$
d. $\frac{2}{5}$

46. Jim was given the following problem to solve. His answer and work are shown below. Circle the part of his work where he made the mistake and then rewrite that step to correct it.

A hardware store sells hammers and saws. The hammers normally cost $25, and the saws are normally $20. This week the hammers are on sale for $5 off, and the saws are on sale for 15% off. If they sell 12 hammers and 14 saws, how many dollars worth of merchandise did they sell?

$$\$25 - \$5 = \$20,\ 20 * 12 = \$240$$

$$\$20 * .15 = \$3,\ \$3 * 14 = \$42$$

$$\$240 + \$42 = \$282$$

____

47. If triangle *ABC* undergoes the following transformations to become triangle *DEF*:

Rotation
Dilation
Reflection

Is triangle *DEF* congruent to triangle *ABC*?

____

Is triangle *DEF* similar to triangle *ABC*?

____

48. At a donut shop, donuts cost $2 per half dozen donuts. Draw a line on the graph below that represents this relationship.

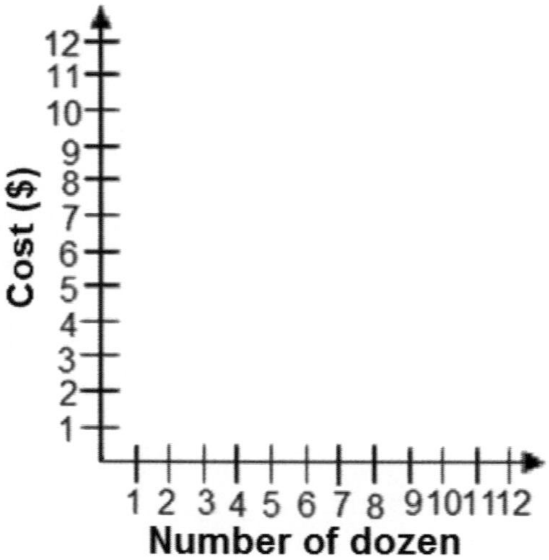

49. If *x*= 3 and *y*= -4, then solve the following equation for *z*. Explain the steps you took to solve the problem.

$$z = (2x + y)x - 3y + x^2$$

____

50. **Gabe was given the following figure with the measurements shown. He was also given a larger figure and told that it was 2.5 times bigger. What are the measurements and area of the larger figure? Figures are not drawn to scale.**

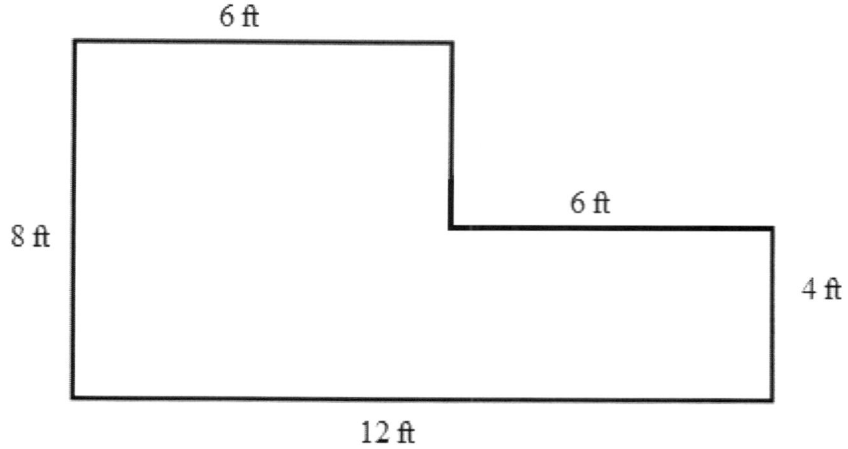

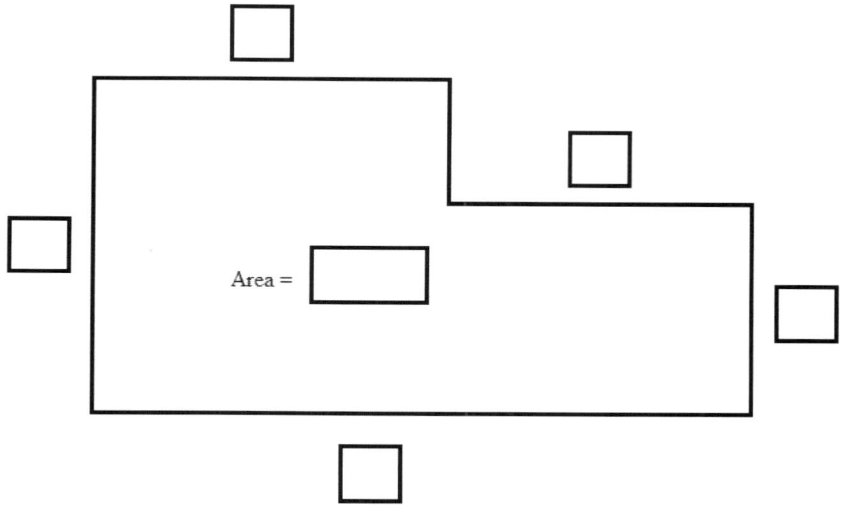

51. Below is part of a neighborhood in Plainville. The school is marked with an *S*. Derrick's house is marked with a *D*, Trent's house is marked with a *T*, and Larry's house is marked with a *L*. The total distance around the park is 1.8 miles. They each walk to school in the morning and then after school they walk from school down to the park and make a lap and return to school. At that point what is the combined distance the three of them have walked since they left home? Plot your answer on the number line below.

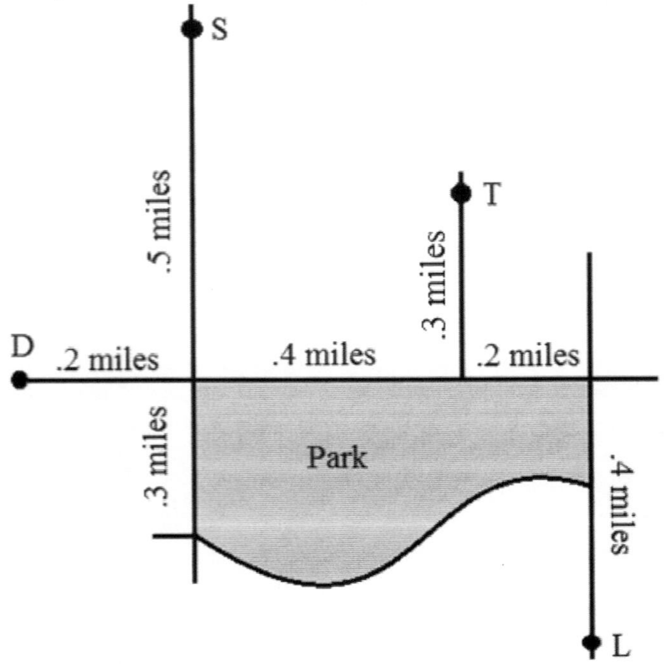

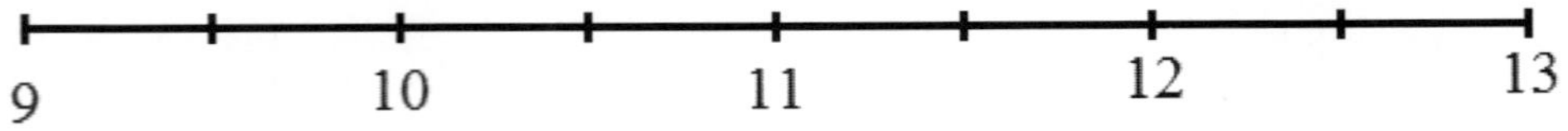

52. **Explain why each of the lines below is or is not a line of symmetry. The dot represents the center of the hexagon.**

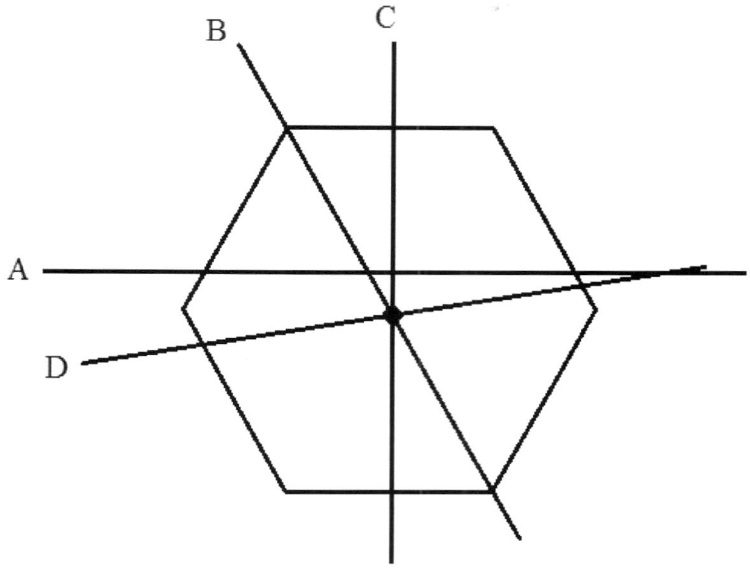

____

____

____

53. **The sphere below represents a water balloon. The shaded area represents the water. It has a radius of 3 inches and has been filled to $\frac{7}{8}$ full. What is the volume of water in the balloon rounded to the nearest hundredth?**

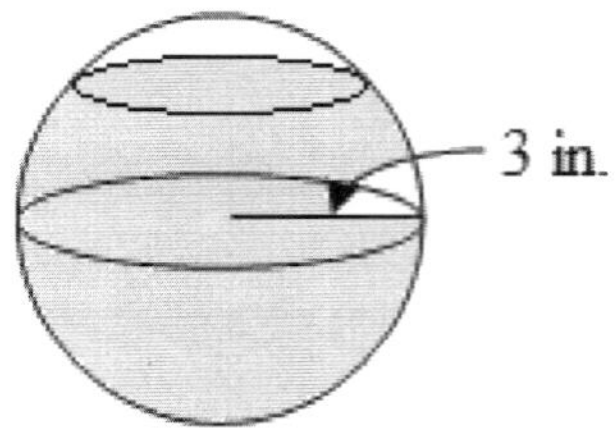

____

Answers and Explanations

1. C: Changing 0.375 into a fraction by writing $\frac{375}{1000}$ because 0.375 is in the thousandths. Then reduce the fraction by dividing the numerator and the denominator by the greatest common factor of 125 to get $\frac{3}{8}$.

2. A: Compare the square of $2\sqrt{5}$ to the square of the whole numbers. $(2\sqrt{5})^2 = 2^2\sqrt{5}^2 = 4 \times 5 = 20$. See that 20 is between 16 and 25, or 4^2 and 5^2, so $2\sqrt{5}$ is between 4 and 5. Checking with a calculator, $2\sqrt{5} \approx 4.472$

3. D: The formula for the area of a square is $A = s^2$, where s is the length of one side of the square. In this case, $64 = s^2$. To solve for s, just square root both sides of the equation and s=8.

4. D: To write a number in scientific notation, the form is $a \times 10^n$, where $1 \leq a < 10$. The decimal need to move 5 spaces to the left so it is immediately to the right of the 3. Because it moved 5 spaces to the left, $n = 5$, so the answer is 3.15×10^5

5. The point on the graph is at (5,1), which shows that after 5 weeks the plant has grown 1 foot. This means that the plant grows $\frac{1}{5}$ft. per week.

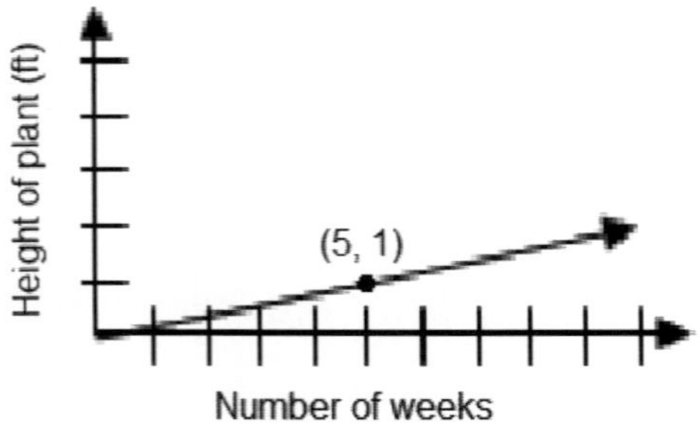

6. C: In both equations, the coefficient of m is the rate of change. In this problem, the rate of change represents the customer's monthly cost. Therefore the customers at John's Gym pay $40 per month, and the customers at Ralph's Recreation Room pay $45 per month. Thus, John's monthly membership fee is less than Ralph's monthly membership fee.

7. A: The slope of a line is its rate of change, or vertical change over horizontal change. For every 2 the line p moves right, it moves up 1. The slope for line p is $\frac{1}{2}$ and the slope of line q is also $\frac{1}{2}$. Therefore, the slope of line p is equal to the slope of line q.

8. C: Dilation of the pentagon by a scale factor of one-third indicates that each dimension of the dilated figure will be one-third that of the dimension in the original figure. Thus, the measurements of the dilated figure can be written as: $9 \cdot \frac{1}{3}$ cm, or 3 cm; $18 \cdot \frac{1}{3}$ cm, or 6 cm; $24 \cdot \frac{1}{3}$ cm, or 8 cm; $18 \cdot \frac{1}{3}$cm, or 6 cm; and $9 \cdot \frac{1}{3}$ cm, or 3 cm.

9. Writing the equation of the line in slope-intercept form $y = mx + b$, the y-intercept, b, is (0,2) and the slope, m, or rate of change is $\frac{1}{1} = 1$. Substituting these numbers into the equation the answer is $y = x + 2$.

10. An example of an equation with no solutions is $6x + 1 = 6x + 3$.

To solve this equation, we can subtract 6x off of both sides. This leaves 3=1 which is not true so there is no solution to this equation.

An example of an equation with one solution is $6x + 1 = 4x + 9$.

The equation is solved below:

$6x + 1 = 4x + 9$ Subtract $4x$ from both sides of the equation
$2x + 1 = 9$ Subtract 1 from both sides of the equation
$2x = 8$ Divide by 2 on both sides of the equation
$x = 4$ So there is one solution to this equation.
An example of an equation with infinite solutions is $6x + 1 = 6x + 1$. For any value of x that is plugged in each side will always equal the other side.

11. A: The equation is solved below:

$2(7x - 5) = 14x - 8$ Distribute 2 across the parentheses
$14x - 10 = 14x - 8$ Subtract $14x$ from both sides of the equation
$-10 = -8$
Because $-10 \neq -8$, no solution exists for the equation.

12. D: The equation is solved below:

$$\frac{1}{2}(x - 7) = \frac{3}{5}(5x + 15)$$

$x - 7 = \frac{6}{5}(5x + 15)$ Clear the fraction $\frac{1}{2}$ on the left by multiplying both sides by 2
$x - 7 = 6x + 18$ Distribute $\frac{6}{5}$ across the parentheses
$-7 = 5x + 18$ Subtract x from both sides
$-25 = 5x$ Subtract 18 from both sides
$-5 = x$ Divide both sides by 5

13. C: The problem is solved below

$$\begin{cases} 2x + y = 7 \\ x - y = 2 \end{cases}$$

$3x = 9$ Because the two equations had opposite terms, add them vertically

$x = 3$ Divide both sides by 3

$2(3) + y = 7$ Substitute 3 into one of the original equations

$6 + y = 7$ Multiply

$y = 1$ Subtract 6 from both sides

(3,1) Write the final answer as an ordered pair (x, y)

14. B: The answer is solved below:

$$\begin{cases} y = -x + 3 \\ y = \frac{1}{2}x + 9 \end{cases}$$

$-x + 3 = \frac{1}{2}x + 9$	Since both expressions are equal to y, set the expressions equal to each other
$3 = \frac{3}{2}x + 9$	Add x to both sides of the equation
$-6 = \frac{3}{2}x$	Subtract 9 from both sides of the equation
$-4 = x$	Multiply both sides by $\frac{2}{3}$
$y = -(-4) + 3$ $= 7$	Substitute the value for x into one of the original equations
$(-4, 7)$	Write the final answer as an ordered pair (x, y)

15. A: The slope is \$0.25, and the y-intercept is –\$18, so the correct steps for finding the profit after selling 49 cookies, will include multiplication of the slope, \$0.25, by the number of cookies, 49, and adding the expenses, or y-intercept, of –18. Thus, you must multiply 49 by \$0.25 and subtract \$18, in order to find the profit.

16. C: The system of linear equation that can be written from the problem is $\begin{cases} \boldsymbol{M + S = 49} \\ \boldsymbol{S = 4M - 1} \end{cases}$.

The solution to the system is below:

M+4M−1=49	Substitute the value for S into the other equation
M+4M−1=49	Remove parentheses
5M−1=49	Combine like terms
5M=50	Add 1 to both sides of the equation
M=10	Divide 5 on both sides of the equation
S=410−1=39	Substitute value of M into other equation and evaluate

Sally sold 39 candy bars.

17. The system of linear equations that can be formed from the problem is $\begin{cases} m + b = 600 \\ m = 5b \end{cases}$. The solution to the system is below:

(5b)+b=600	Substitute the expression for m into the other equation
5b+b=600	Remove parentheses
6b=600	Combine like terms
b=100	Divide by 6 on both sides
m=5100=500	Substitute the value for b into the expression for m and evaluate.

So, the final equation would be $500 + 100 = 600$

18. D: A function cannot map a single input to more than one output. The vertical line test states that if a vertical line touches a graph in more than one point, then it is not a function. The graph from answer D does not pass the vertical line test so it is not a function.

19. Image A could be translated, rotated, or reflected to form image B. It cannot be dilated to form image B. A translation is just "sliding" an image to a new location. A reflection makes a mirror image on the other side of a line of reflection. A rotation just turns the image. It cannot be dialted because that would change the size of the image.

20. D: The number of miles Kevin drives per hour can be written as $y = 65x$, where x represents the number of hours and y represents the total number of miles driven. The y-intercept is 0, since there is not an amount added to, or subtracted from, this term. The graph of the line passes through the origin, or the point, (0, 0).

21. A: The range of the function is the set of all outputs, or y-values. The range of Function I is from−4 to 2, and the range of Function II is the set of all real numbers. Therefore the range of Function I is smaller than the range of Function II.

22. D: A function is linear if the powers of the x and y variables are 1. In answer D, the $\sqrt{x} = x^{1/2}$, so its exponent is not 1, thus answer D is not linear.

23. First find the y-intercept, which is where $x = 0$. In this case it is -2. Next, find the slope of the line. Slope is equal to rise over run, or in this case $\frac{10}{2} = 5$. So, the equation in slope intercept form is y=5x-2.

24. C: Since the triangles are similar, $\overline{AB} = \overline{DE}$ and $\overline{AC} = \overline{DF}$. Thus, The proportion can be written as: $\frac{18}{27} = \frac{11}{x}$. Solving for x gives: $18x = 297$, or $x = 16.5$. Thus, $\overline{DF}$ is 16.5 inches, in length.

25. B: The equations are in slope-intercept form. The y-intercept, b, is the point where the graph touches the y-axis. The y-intercept of this graph is $(0, -3)$. The slope, m, is the vertical change over the horizontal change. The vertical change is 3 and the horizontal change is 1 so the slope is $\frac{3}{1} = 3$. Substituting these numbers into the slope-intercept form you will get $y = 3x - 3$.

26. On a graph, a function is increasing if the line is sloping up as it is moving from left to right. The only interval on the graph with positive slope is $2 < x < 3$.

27. A: As the bike rolls down the hill, the speed gradually increases. When the pedaling then moves to a constant rate, the speed will reach a constant rate shown by a horizontal line. When the bike stops at a store, the speed then drops to the x-axis. The only graph that shows all three parts is answer A.

28. A: A rotation, or turn, is only seen in answer A. Answer B shows a translation, or slide; answer C shows a dilation; and answer C shows a reflection or translation.

29. B: A cylinder with a height of 9 inches and radius of 4 inches has a volume equal to $\pi(4)^2(9)$ cubic inches, or approximately 452.16 cubic inches. A cylinder with a height of 9 inches and a radius of 12 inches has a volume equal to $\pi(12)^2(9)$ cubic inches, or approximately 4,069.44 cubic inches. The volume of the second cylinder is 9 times larger than the volume of the original cylinder.

30. They represent a dilation. The shapes are congruent, one is just bigger than the other.

31. D: If a dilation has a scale factor if 3, then the length of each side is multiplied by 3 to get the new length. The measure of $\overline{AB}$ is 6, so when it is multiplied by 3 it becomes 18.

32. C: Because the two figures are different sizes, one of the transformations is a dilation. Also, the figures are turned which is a rotation. Answer C gives those two answers.

33. D: The Triangle Sum Theorem says the three angles of a triangle must add up to **180°.**

So $60° + 40° + m\angle A = 180°$
$100° + m\angle A = 180°$ Combine like terms
$m\angle A = 80°$ Subtract 105 from both sides

34. A: First solve for BC. By use of the Pythagorean Theorem $a^2 + b^2 = c^2$ and substituting the appropriate values, the equation becomes

$BC^2 + 40^2 = 41^2$
$BC^2 + 1600 = 1681$ Evaluate the exponents
$BC^2 = 81$ Subtract 1600 from both sides
$BC = 9$ Take the square root of both sides

To find how much more $AB + BC$ is compared to AC evaluate the expression $(AB + BC) - AC$. This yields $(40 + 9) - 41 = 8$.

35. The distance formula is $d = \sqrt{(x_2 - x_1)^2 + (y_2 - y_1)^2}$, and plugging in values then evaluating will get the final answer.

$$\sqrt{\left(-6-(-3)\right)^2 + (9-1)^2}$$
$$\sqrt{(-3)^2 + 8^2}$$
$$\sqrt{9+64}$$
$$\sqrt{73} \approx 8.54$$

36. C: The probability of independent events, A and B, can be found, by using the formula, $P(A\ and\ B) = P(A) \cdot P(B)$. Thus, the probability can be written as $\frac{1}{2} \cdot \frac{4}{52}$, or $\frac{4}{104}$, which reduces to $\frac{1}{26}$.

37. A: The volume formula for a rectangular solid is $V = lwh$. In this problem the volume is 48 cu. inches. So, and three numbers that multiply to be 48 would work. An example is given below.

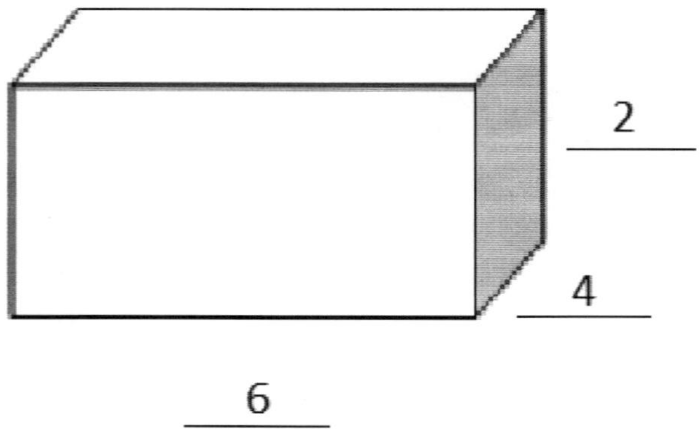

2 ∗ 4 ∗ 6 = 48

38. A: The reflection of a figure about the x-axis requires the negation of the y-value. The vertices of the given triangle are (3, 9), (2, 4), and (6, 2). Thus, the vertices of the triangle, reflected about the x-axis, are (3, −9), (2, −4), and (6, −2).

39. B: The volume formula for a sphere is $V = \frac{4}{3}\pi r^3$. Plugging in the value of the radius then evaluating will yield the final answer:

$$V = \frac{4}{3}(3.14)(12\ yd)^3$$
$$V = 7234.56\ yd^3$$

40. C: If a line is drawn as close to the points as possible, the y-intercept would be 7 and the slope would be -1. From this information, the line is $y = -x + 7$

41. B: If a line-of-fit is drawn through the points, the slope will be $-\frac{1}{5}$ so the snow melts 5 centimeters every day.

42. The percentage of women with blue eyes is $\frac{20}{80} = 25\%$, and the percentage of men with blue eyes is $\frac{15}{95} \approx 15.8\%$ .Therefore a larger percentage of women surveyed have blue eyes then the percentage men who were surveyed that have blue eyes, and the statement is true.

43. We know that Jaime is 9, and Brett is 2 years older, so he must be 11. Susie is 4 years younger than twice Brett, so she is 18. Then Blake is 3 years younger, so he is 15. The number line should look like this.

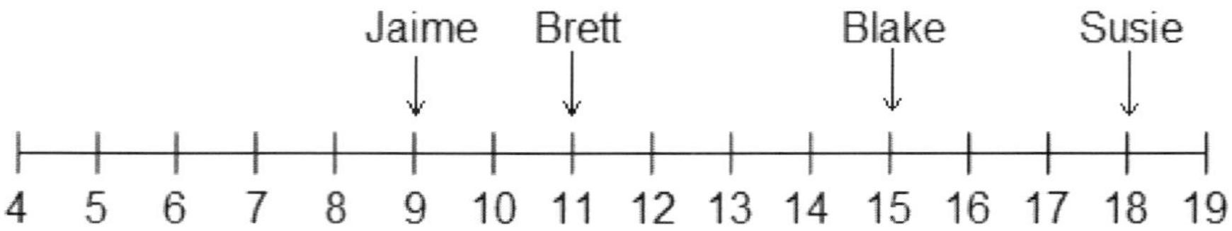

44. B: The lateral surface area of a cylinder can be determined by evaluating the expression, $2\pi rh$, where r represents the radius and h represents the height of the cylinder. Substituting the radius of 8 inches and the height of 14 inches allows you to write: $2\pi(8)(14)$, which is approximately 703.36. Thus, the lateral surface area of the cylinder is approximately 703.36 square inches.

45. C: The probability of a coin landing on heads is $\frac{1}{2}$. The probability of two dice landing on 10 or better is $\frac{3}{12}$. To find the probaility of both multiply them together. So, $\frac{1}{2} * \frac{3}{12} = \frac{3}{24} = \frac{1}{8}$.

46. The place where he made a mistake was when he applied the 15% discount to the saws. He wrote $\$20 * .15 = \$3$, but they are 15% off not 15% of the original cost. So, it should be $\$20 * .85 = \$3$.

47. For two shapes to be congruent they must be the same size and same shape. If the triangle undergoes a dilation it is no longer congruent. So, triangle *DEF* is not congruen to triangle *ABC*. For two shapes to be similar they just have to be the same shape but the size can be different. In, this case triangle *DEF* is similar to triangle *ABC*.

48. If donuts are \$2 per half dozen, then they are \$4 per dozen. The graph below represents this relationship.

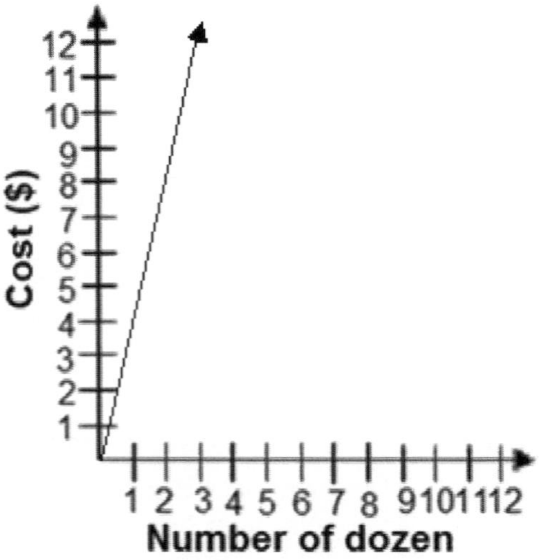

49. The first step is to plug in the values for *x* and *y*. This gives $\left(2(3)+(-4)\right)(3)-3(-4)+(3)^2$. Next, follow the order of operations to solve.

$$z=(2)(3)-3(-4)+(3)^2=$$
$$(2)(3)-3(-4)+9=$$
$$6+12+9=27$$

50. First multiply all of the side measures by 2.5 to get the side measures of the larger figure. Next treat the figure like to separate rectangles to find the area. One would be 15ft by 20 ft and the other would be 15ft by 10 ft. Then find the area of each and add them together. So, $15\times 20=300$, $15\times 10=150$, and $300+150=450$.

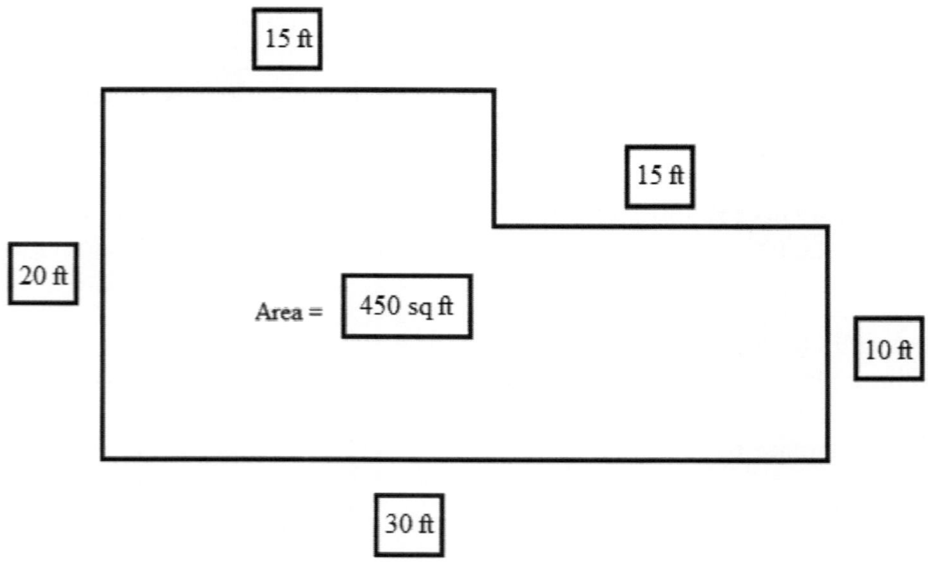

51. 11.8: First add the distance that it takes for each one to walk to school. Derrick walks .7 miles, Trent walks 1.2 miles, and Larry walks 1.5 miles. Then after school they each walk .5 miles back to the park and then make one lap which is 1.8 miles and then walk .5 miles back to the school. That's

2.8 miles per person times 3 people. So, add them all up to get $.7 + 1.2 + 1.5 + 2.8 + 2.8 + 2.8 = 11.8$. Then plot the point on the number line.

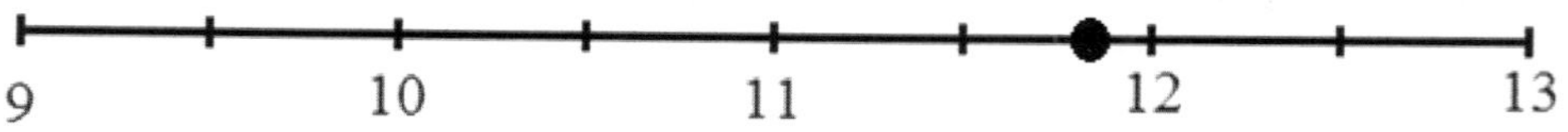

52. A line of symmetry is a line that divides a figure into two congruent parts. In the hexagon given only line B and C would divide the hexagon into two congruent halves.

53. 98.96 cubic in.: The formula for volume of a sphere is $\frac{4}{3}\pi r^3$. Plug in 3 inches for the radius and solve to get 113.09734. Then to find the just the volume of the water multiply that time $\frac{7}{8}$ or .875. 113.09734(.875)= 98.96.

How to Overcome Test Anxiety

Just the thought of taking a test is enough to make most people a little nervous. A test is an important event that can have a long-term impact on your future, so it's important to take it seriously and it's natural to feel anxious about performing well. But just because anxiety is normal, that doesn't mean that it's helpful in test taking, or that you should simply accept it as part of your life. Anxiety can have a variety of effects. These effects can be mild, like making you feel slightly nervous, or severe, like blocking your ability to focus or remember even a simple detail.

If you experience test anxiety—whether severe or mild—it's important to know how to beat it. To discover this, first you need to understand what causes test anxiety.

Causes of Test Anxiety

While we often think of anxiety as an uncontrollable emotional state, it can actually be caused by simple, practical things. One of the most common causes of test anxiety is that a person does not feel adequately prepared for their test. This feeling can be the result of many different issues such as poor study habits or lack of organization, but the most common culprit is time management. Starting to study too late, failing to organize your study time to cover all of the material, or being distracted while you study will mean that you're not well prepared for the test. This may lead to cramming the night before, which will cause you to be physically and mentally exhausted for the test. Poor time management also contributes to feelings of stress, fear, and hopelessness as you realize you are not well prepared but don't know what to do about it.

Other times, test anxiety is not related to your preparation for the test but comes from unresolved fear. This may be a past failure on a test, or poor performance on tests in general. It may come from comparing yourself to others who seem to be performing better or from the stress of living up to expectations. Anxiety may be driven by fears of the future—how failure on this test would affect your educational and career goals. These fears are often completely irrational, but they can still negatively impact your test performance.

Elements of Test Anxiety

As mentioned earlier, test anxiety is considered to be an emotional state, but it has physical and mental components as well. Sometimes you may not even realize that you are suffering from test anxiety until you notice the physical symptoms. These can include trembling hands, rapid heartbeat, sweating, nausea, and tense muscles. Extreme anxiety may lead to fainting or vomiting. Obviously, any of these symptoms can have a negative impact on testing. It is important to recognize them as soon as they begin to occur so that you can address the problem before it damages your performance.

The mental components of test anxiety include trouble focusing and inability to remember learned information. During a test, your mind is on high alert, which can help you recall information and stay focused for an extended period of time. However, anxiety interferes with your mind's natural processes, causing you to blank out, even on the questions you know well. The strain of testing during anxiety makes it difficult to stay focused, especially on a test that may take several hours. Extreme anxiety can take a huge mental toll, making it difficult not only to recall test information but even to understand the test questions or pull your thoughts together.

Effects of Test Anxiety

Test anxiety is like a disease—if left untreated, it will get progressively worse. Anxiety leads to poor performance, and this reinforces the feelings of fear and failure, which in turn lead to poor performances on subsequent tests. It can grow from a mild nervousness to a crippling condition. If allowed to progress, test anxiety can have a big impact on your schooling, and consequently on your future.

Test anxiety can spread to other parts of your life. Anxiety on tests can become anxiety in any stressful situation, and blanking on a test can turn into panicking in a job situation. But fortunately, you don't have to let anxiety rule your testing and determine your grades. There are a number of relatively simple steps you can take to move past anxiety and function normally on a test and in the rest of life.

Physical Steps for Beating Test Anxiety

While test anxiety is a serious problem, the good news is that it can be overcome. It doesn't have to control your ability to think and remember information. While it may take time, you can begin taking steps today to beat anxiety.

Just as your first hint that you may be struggling with anxiety comes from the physical symptoms, the first step to treating it is also physical. Rest is crucial for having a clear, strong mind. If you are tired, it is much easier to give in to anxiety. But if you establish good sleep habits, your body and mind will be ready to perform optimally, without the strain of exhaustion. Additionally, sleeping well helps you to retain information better, so you're more likely to recall the answers when you see the test questions.

Getting good sleep means more than going to bed on time. It's important to allow your brain time to relax. Take study breaks from time to time so it doesn't get overworked, and don't study right before bed. Take time to rest your mind before trying to rest your body, or you may find it difficult to fall asleep.

Along with sleep, other aspects of physical health are important in preparing for a test. Good nutrition is vital for good brain function. Sugary foods and drinks may give a burst of energy but this burst is followed by a crash, both physically and emotionally. Instead, fuel your body with protein and vitamin-rich foods.

Also, drink plenty of water. Dehydration can lead to headaches and exhaustion, especially if your brain is already under stress from the rigors of the test. Particularly if your test is a long one, drink water during the breaks. And if possible, take an energy-boosting snack to eat between sections.

Along with sleep and diet, a third important part of physical health is exercise. Maintaining a steady workout schedule is helpful, but even taking 5-minute study breaks to walk can help get your blood pumping faster and clear your head. Exercise also releases endorphins, which contribute to a positive feeling and can help combat test anxiety.

When you nurture your physical health, you are also contributing to your mental health. If your body is healthy, your mind is much more likely to be healthy as well. So take time to rest, nourish your body with healthy food and water, and get moving as much as possible. Taking these physical steps will make you stronger and more able to take the mental steps necessary to overcome test anxiety.

Mental Steps for Beating Test Anxiety

Working on the mental side of test anxiety can be more challenging, but as with the physical side, there are clear steps you can take to overcome it. As mentioned earlier, test anxiety often stems from lack of preparation, so the obvious solution is to prepare for the test. Effective studying may be the most important weapon you have for beating test anxiety, but you can and should employ several other mental tools to combat fear.

First, boost your confidence by reminding yourself of past success—tests or projects that you aced. If you're putting as much effort into preparing for this test as you did for those, there's no reason you should expect to fail here. Work hard to prepare; then trust your preparation.

Second, surround yourself with encouraging people. It can be helpful to find a study group, but be sure that the people you're around will encourage a positive attitude. If you spend time with others who are anxious or cynical, this will only contribute to your own anxiety. Look for others who are motivated to study hard from a desire to succeed, not from a fear of failure.

Third, reward yourself. A test is physically and mentally tiring, even without anxiety, and it can be helpful to have something to look forward to. Plan an activity following the test, regardless of the outcome, such as going to a movie or getting ice cream.

When you are taking the test, if you find yourself beginning to feel anxious, remind yourself that you know the material. Visualize successfully completing the test. Then take a few deep, relaxing breaths and return to it. Work through the questions carefully but with confidence, knowing that you are capable of succeeding.

Developing a healthy mental approach to test taking will also aid in other areas of life. Test anxiety affects more than just the actual test—it can be damaging to your mental health and even contribute to depression. It's important to beat test anxiety before it becomes a problem for more than testing.

Study Strategy

Being prepared for the test is necessary to combat anxiety, but what does being prepared look like? You may study for hours on end and still not feel prepared. What you need is a strategy for test prep. The next few pages outline our recommended steps to help you plan out and conquer the challenge of preparation.

Step 1: Scope Out the Test

Learn everything you can about the format (multiple choice, essay, etc.) and what will be on the test. Gather any study materials, course outlines, or sample exams that may be available. Not only will this help you to prepare, but knowing what to expect can help to alleviate test anxiety.

Step 2: Map Out the Material

Look through the textbook or study guide and make note of how many chapters or sections it has. Then divide these over the time you have. For example, if a book has 15 chapters and you have five days to study, you need to cover three chapters each day. Even better, if you have the time, leave an extra day at the end for overall review after you have gone through the material in depth.

If time is limited, you may need to prioritize the material. Look through it and make note of which sections you think you already have a good grasp on, and which need review. While you are studying, skim quickly through the familiar sections and take more time on the challenging parts.

Write out your plan so you don't get lost as you go. Having a written plan also helps you feel more in control of the study, so anxiety is less likely to arise from feeling overwhelmed at the amount to cover.

Step 3: Gather Your Tools

Decide what study method works best for you. Do you prefer to highlight in the book as you study and then go back over the highlighted portions? Or do you type out notes of the important information? Or is it helpful to make flashcards that you can carry with you? Assemble the pens, index cards, highlighters, post-it notes, and any other materials you may need so you won't be distracted by getting up to find things while you study.

If you're having a hard time retaining the information or organizing your notes, experiment with different methods. For example, try color-coding by subject with colored pens, highlighters, or post-it notes. If you learn better by hearing, try recording yourself reading your notes so you can listen while in the car, working out, or simply sitting at your desk. Ask a friend to quiz you from your flashcards, or try teaching someone the material to solidify it in your mind.

Step 4: Create Your Environment

It's important to avoid distractions while you study. This includes both the obvious distractions like visitors and the subtle distractions like an uncomfortable chair (or a too-comfortable couch that makes you want to fall asleep). Set up the best study environment possible: good lighting and a comfortable work area. If background music helps you focus, you may want to turn it on, but otherwise keep the room quiet. If you are using a computer to take notes, be sure you don't have any other windows open, especially applications like social media, games, or anything else that could distract you. Silence your phone and turn off notifications. Be sure to keep water close by so you stay hydrated while you study (but avoid unhealthy drinks and snacks).

Also, take into account the best time of day to study. Are you freshest first thing in the morning? Try to set aside some time then to work through the material. Is your mind clearer in the afternoon or evening? Schedule your study session then. Another method is to study at the same time of day that you will take the test, so that your brain gets used to working on the material at that time and will be ready to focus at test time.

Step 5: Study!

Once you have done all the study preparation, it's time to settle into the actual studying. Sit down, take a few moments to settle your mind so you can focus, and begin to follow your study plan. Don't give in to distractions or let yourself procrastinate. This is your time to prepare so you'll be ready to fearlessly approach the test. Make the most of the time and stay focused.

Of course, you don't want to burn out. If you study too long you may find that you're not retaining the information very well. Take regular study breaks. For example, taking five minutes out of every hour to walk briskly, breathing deeply and swinging your arms, can help your mind stay fresh.

As you get to the end of each chapter or section, it's a good idea to do a quick review. Remind yourself of what you learned and work on any difficult parts. When you feel that you've mastered the material, move on to the next part. At the end of your study session, briefly skim through your notes again.

But while review is helpful, cramming last minute is NOT. If at all possible, work ahead so that you won't need to fit all your study into the last day. Cramming overloads your brain with more information than it can process and retain, and your tired mind may struggle to recall even previously learned information when it is overwhelmed with last-minute study. Also, the urgent nature of cramming and the stress placed on your brain contribute to anxiety. You'll be more likely to go to the test feeling unprepared and having trouble thinking clearly.

So don't cram, and don't stay up late before the test, even just to review your notes at a leisurely pace. Your brain needs rest more than it needs to go over the information again. In fact, plan to finish your studies by noon or early afternoon the day before the test. Give your brain the rest of the day to relax or focus on other things, and get a good night's sleep. Then you will be fresh for the test and better able to recall what you've studied.

Step 6: Take a Practice Test

Many courses offer sample tests, either online or in the study materials. This is an excellent resource to check whether you have mastered the material, as well as to prepare for the test format and environment.

Check the test format ahead of time: the number of questions, the type (multiple choice, free response, etc.), and the time limit. Then create a plan for working through them. For example, if you have 30 minutes to take a 60-question test, your limit is 30 seconds per question. Spend less time on the questions you know well so that you can take more time on the difficult ones.

If you have time to take several practice tests, take the first one open book, with no time limit. Work through the questions at your own pace and make sure you fully understand them. Gradually work up to taking a test under test conditions: sit at a desk with all study materials put away and set a timer. Pace yourself to make sure you finish the test with time to spare and go back to check your answers if you have time.

After each test, check your answers. On the questions you missed, be sure you understand why you missed them. Did you misread the question (tests can use tricky wording)? Did you forget the information? Or was it something you hadn't learned? Go back and study any shaky areas that the practice tests reveal.

Taking these tests not only helps with your grade, but also aids in combating test anxiety. If you're already used to the test conditions, you're less likely to worry about it, and working through tests until you're scoring well gives you a confidence boost. Go through the practice tests until you feel comfortable, and then you can go into the test knowing that you're ready for it.

Test Tips

On test day, you should be confident, knowing that you've prepared well and are ready to answer the questions. But aside from preparation, there are several test day strategies you can employ to maximize your performance.

First, as stated before, get a good night's sleep the night before the test (and for several nights before that, if possible). Go into the test with a fresh, alert mind rather than staying up late to study.

Try not to change too much about your normal routine on the day of the test. It's important to eat a nutritious breakfast, but if you normally don't eat breakfast at all, consider eating just a protein bar. If you're a coffee drinker, go ahead and have your normal coffee. Just make sure you time it so that the caffeine doesn't wear off right in the middle of your test. Avoid sugary beverages, and drink enough water to stay hydrated but not so much that you need a restroom break 10 minutes into the test. If your test isn't first thing in the morning, consider going for a walk or doing a light workout before the test to get your blood flowing.

Allow yourself enough time to get ready, and leave for the test with plenty of time to spare so you won't have the anxiety of scrambling to arrive in time. Another reason to be early is to select a good seat. It's helpful to sit away from doors and windows, which can be distracting. Find a good seat, get out your supplies, and settle your mind before the test begins.

When the test begins, start by going over the instructions carefully, even if you already know what to expect. Make sure you avoid any careless mistakes by following the directions.

Then begin working through the questions, pacing yourself as you've practiced. If you're not sure on an answer, don't spend too much time on it, and don't let it shake your confidence. Either skip it and come back later, or eliminate as many wrong answers as possible and guess among the remaining ones. Don't dwell on these questions as you continue—put them out of your mind and focus on what lies ahead.

Be sure to read all of the answer choices, even if you're sure the first one is the right answer. Sometimes you'll find a better one if you keep reading. But don't second-guess yourself if you do immediately know the answer. Your gut instinct is usually right. Don't let test anxiety rob you of the information you know.

If you have time at the end of the test (and if the test format allows), go back and review your answers. Be cautious about changing any, since your first instinct tends to be correct, but make sure you didn't misread any of the questions or accidentally mark the wrong answer choice. Look over any you skipped and make an educated guess.

At the end, leave the test feeling confident. You've done your best, so don't waste time worrying about your performance or wishing you could change anything. Instead, celebrate the successful completion of this test. And finally, use this test to learn how to deal with anxiety even better next time.

Review Video: Test Anxiety
Visit mometrix.com/academy and enter code: 100340

Important Qualification

Not all anxiety is created equal. If your test anxiety is causing major issues in your life beyond the classroom or testing center, or if you are experiencing troubling physical symptoms related to your anxiety, it may be a sign of a serious physiological or psychological condition. If this sounds like your situation, we strongly encourage you to seek professional help.

How to Overcome Your Fear of Math

Not again. You're sitting in math class, look down at your test, and immediately start to panic. Your stomach is in knots, your heart is racing, and you break out in a cold sweat. You're staring at the paper, but everything looks like it's written in a foreign language. Even though you studied, you're blanking out on how to begin solving these problems.

Does this sound familiar? If so, then you're not alone! You may be like millions of other people who experience math anxiety. Anxiety about performing well in math is a common experience for students of all ages. In this article, we'll discuss what math anxiety is, common misconceptions about learning math, and tips and strategies for overcoming math anxiety.

What Is Math Anxiety?

Psychologist Mark H. Ashcraft explains math anxiety as a feeling of tension, apprehension, or fear that interferes with math performance. Having math anxiety negatively impacts people's beliefs about themselves and what they can achieve. It hinders achievement within the math classroom and affects the successful application of mathematics in the real world.

Symptoms and Signs of Math Anxiety

To overcome math anxiety, you must recognize its symptoms. Becoming aware of the signs of math anxiety is the first step in addressing and resolving these fears.

Negative Self-Talk

If you have math anxiety, you've most likely said at least one of these statements to yourself:

- "I hate math."
- "I'm not good at math."
- "I'm not a math person."

The way we speak to ourselves and think about ourselves matters. Our thoughts become our words, our words become our actions, and our actions become our habits. Thinking negatively about math creates a self-fulfilling prophecy. In other words, if you take an idea as a fact, then it will come true because your behaviors will align to match it.

Avoidance

Some people who are fearful or anxious about math will tend to avoid it altogether. Avoidance can manifest in the following ways:

- Lack of engagement with math content
- Not completing homework and other assignments
- Not asking for help when needed
- Skipping class
- Avoiding math-related courses and activities

Avoidance is one of the most harmful impacts of math anxiety. If you steer clear of math at all costs, then you can't set yourself up for the success you deserve.

Lack of Motivation

Students with math anxiety may experience a lack of motivation. They may struggle to find the incentive to get engaged with what they view as a frightening subject. These students are often overwhelmed, making it difficult for them to complete or even start math assignments.

Procrastination

Another symptom of math anxiety is procrastination. Students may voluntarily delay or postpone their classwork and assignments, even if they know there will be a negative consequence for doing so. Additionally, they may choose to wait until the last minute to start projects and homework, even when they know they need more time to put forth their best effort.

Physiological Reactions

Many people with a fear of math experience physiological side effects. These may include an increase in heart rate, sweatiness, shakiness, nausea, and irregular breathing. These symptoms make it difficult to focus on the math content, causing the student even more stress and fear.

Strong Emotional Responses

Math anxiety also affects people on an emotional level. Responding to math content with strong emotions such as panic, anger, or despair can be a sign of math anxiety.

Low Test Scores and Performance

Low achievement can be both a symptom and a cause of math anxiety. When someone does not take the steps needed to perform well on tests and assessments, they are less likely to pass. The more they perform poorly, the more they accept this poor performance as a fact that can't be changed.

Feeling Alone

People who experience math anxiety feel like they are the only ones struggling, even if the math they are working on is challenging to many people. Feeling isolated in what they perceive as failure can trigger tension or nervousness.

Feeling of Permanency

Math anxiety can feel very permanent. You may assume that you are naturally bad at math and always will be. Viewing math as a natural ability rather than a skill that can be learned causes people to believe that nothing will help them improve. They take their current math abilities as fact and assume that they can't be changed. As a result, they give up, stop trying to improve, and avoid engaging with math altogether.

Lack of Confidence

People with low self-confidence in math tend to feel awkward and incompetent when asked to solve a math problem. They don't feel comfortable taking chances or risks when problem-solving because they second-guess themselves and assume they are incorrect. They don't trust in their ability to learn the content and solve problems correctly.

Panic

A general sense of unexplained panic is also a sign of math anxiety. You may feel a sudden sense of fear that triggers physical reactions, even when there is no apparent reason for such a response.

Causes Of Math Anxiety

Math anxiety can start at a young age and may have one or more underlying causes. Common causes of math anxiety include the following:

The Attitude of Parents or Guardians

Parents often put pressure on their children to perform well in school. Although their intentions are usually good, this pressure can lead to anxiety, especially if the student is struggling with a subject or class.

Perhaps your parents or others in your life hold negative predispositions about math based on their own experiences. For instance, if your mother once claimed she was not good at math, then you might have incorrectly interpreted this as a predisposed trait that was passed down to you.

Teacher Influence

Students often pick up on their teachers' attitudes about the content being taught. If a teacher is happy and excited about math, students are more likely to mirror these emotions. However, if a teacher lacks enthusiasm or genuine interest, then students are more inclined to disengage.

Teachers have a responsibility to cultivate a welcoming classroom culture that is accepting of mistakes. When teachers blame students for not understanding a concept, they create a hostile classroom environment where mistakes are not tolerated. This tension increases student stress and anxiety, creating conditions that are not conducive to inquiry and learning. Instead, when teachers normalize mistakes as a natural part of the problem-solving process, they give their students the freedom to explore and grapple with the math content. In such an environment, students feel comfortable taking chances because they are not afraid of being wrong.

Students need teachers that can help when they're having problems understanding difficult concepts. In doing so, educators may need to change how they teach the content. Since different people have unique learning styles, it's the job of the teacher to adapt to the needs of each student. Additionally, teachers should encourage students to explore alternate problem-solving strategies, even if it's not the preferred method of the educator.

Fear of Being Wrong

Embarrassing situations can be traumatic, especially for young children and adolescents. These experiences can stay with people through their adult lives. Those with math anxiety may experience a fear of being wrong, especially in front of a group of peers. This fear can be paralyzing, interfering with the student's concentration and ability to focus on the problem at hand.

Timed Assessments

Timed assessments can help improve math fluency, but they often create unnecessary pressure for students to complete an unrealistic number of problems within a specified timeframe. Many studies have shown that timed assessments often result in increased levels of anxiety, reducing a student's overall competence and ability to problem-solve.

Debunking Math Myths

There are lots of myths about math that are related to the causes and development of math-related anxiety. Although these myths have been proven to be false, many people take them as fact. Let's go over a few of the most common myths about learning math.

Myth: Men Are Better at Math Than Women

Math has a reputation for being a male-dominant subject, but this doesn't mean that men are inherently better at math than women. Many famous mathematical discoveries have been made by women. Katherine Johnson, Dame Mary Lucy Cartwright, and Marjorie Lee Brown are just a few of the many famous women mathematicians. Expecting to be good or bad at math because of your gender sets you up for stress and confusion. Math is a skill that can be learned, just like cooking or riding a bike.

Myth: There Is Only One Good Way to Solve Math Problems

There are many ways to get the correct answer when it comes to math. No two people have the same brain, so everyone takes a slightly different approach to problem-solving. Moreover, there isn't one way of problem-solving that's superior to another. Your way of working through a problem might differ from someone else's, and that is okay. Math can be a highly individualized process, so the best method for you should be the one that makes you feel the most comfortable and makes the most sense to you.

Myth: Math Requires a Good Memory

For many years, mathematics was taught through memorization. However, learning in such a way hinders the development of critical thinking and conceptual understanding. These skill sets are much more valuable than basic memorization. For instance, you might be great at memorizing mathematical formulas, but if you don't understand what they mean, then you can't apply them to different scenarios in the real world. When a student is working from memory, they are limited in the strategies available to them to problem-solve. In other words, they assume there is only one correct way to do the math, which is the method they memorized. Having a variety of problem-solving options can help students figure out which method works best for them. Additionally, it provides students with a better understanding of how and why certain mathematical strategies work. While memorization can be helpful in some instances, it is not an absolute requirement for mathematicians.

Myth: Math Is Not Creative

Math requires imagination and intuition. Contrary to popular belief, it is a highly creative field. Mathematical creativity can help in developing new ways to think about and solve problems. Many people incorrectly assume that all things are either creative or analytical. However, this black-and-white view is limiting because the field of mathematics involves both creativity and logic.

Myth: Math Isn't Supposed To Be Fun

Whoever told you that math isn't supposed to be fun is a liar. There are tons of math-based activities and games that foster friendly competition and engagement. Math is often best learned through play, and lots of mobile apps and computer games exemplify this.

Additionally, math can be an exceptionally collaborative and social experience. Studying or working through problems with a friend often makes the process a lot more fun. The excitement and satisfaction of solving a difficult problem with others is quite rewarding. Math can be fun if you look for ways to make it more collaborative and enjoyable.

Myth: Not Everyone Is Capable of Learning Math

There's no such thing as a "math person." Although many people think that you're either good at math or you're not, this is simply not true. Everyone is capable of learning and applying mathematics. However, not everyone learns the same way. Since each person has a different learning style, the trick is to find the strategies and learning tools that work best for you. Some people learn best through hands-on experiences, and others find success through the use of visual aids. Others are auditory learners and learn best by hearing and listening. When people are overwhelmed or feel that math is too hard, it's often because they haven't found the learning strategy that works best for them.

Myth: Good Mathematicians Work Quickly and Never Make Mistakes

There is no prize for finishing first in math. It's not a race, and speed isn't a measure of your ability. Good mathematicians take their time to ensure their work is accurate. As you gain more experience and practice, you will naturally become faster and more confident.

Additionally, everyone makes mistakes, including good mathematicians. Mistakes are a normal part of the problem-solving process, and they're not a bad thing. The important thing is that we take the time to learn from our mistakes, understand where our misconceptions are, and move forward.

Myth: You Don't Need Math in the Real World

Our day-to-day lives are so infused with mathematical concepts that we often don't even realize when we're using math in the real world. In fact, most people tend to underestimate how much we do math in our everyday lives. It's involved in an enormous variety of daily activities such as shopping, baking, finances, and gardening, as well as in many careers, including architecture, nursing, design, and sales.

Tips and Strategies for Overcoming Math Anxiety

If your anxiety is getting in the way of your level of mathematical engagement, then there are lots of steps you can take. Check out the strategies below to start building confidence in math today.

Focus on Understanding, Not Memorization

Don't drive yourself crazy trying to memorize every single formula or mathematical process. Instead, shift your attention to understanding concepts. Those who prioritize memorization over conceptual understanding tend to have lower achievement levels in math. Students who memorize may be able to complete some math, but they don't understand the process well enough to apply it to different situations. Memorization comes with time and practice, but it won't help alleviate math anxiety. On the other hand, conceptual understanding will give you the building blocks of knowledge you need to build up your confidence.

Replace Negative Self-Talk with Positive Self-Talk

Start to notice how you think about yourself. Whenever you catch yourself thinking something negative, try replacing that thought with a positive affirmation. Instead of continuing the negative thought, pause to reframe the situation. For ideas on how to get started, take a look at the table below:

Instead of thinking...	Try thinking...
"I can't do this math." "I'm not a math person."	"I'm up for the challenge, and I'm training my brain in math."
"This problem is too hard."	"This problem is hard, so this might take some time and effort. I know I can do this."
"I give up."	"What strategies can help me solve this problem?"
"I made a mistake, so I'm not good at this."	"Everyone makes mistakes. Mistakes help me to grow and understand."
"I'll never be smart enough."	"I can figure this out, and I am smart enough."

Practice Mindfulness

Practicing mindfulness and focusing on your breathing can help alleviate some of the physical symptoms of math anxiety. By taking deep breaths, you can remind your nervous system that you are not in immediate danger. Doing so will reduce your heart rate and help with any irregular breathing or shakiness. Taking the edge off of the physiological effects of anxiety will clear your mind, allowing your brain to focus its energy on problem-solving.

Do Some Math Every Day

Think about learning math as if you were learning a foreign language. If you don't use it, you lose it. If you don't practice your math skills regularly, you'll have a harder time achieving comprehension and fluency. Set some amount of time aside each day, even if it's just for a few minutes, to practice. It might take some discipline to build a habit around this, but doing so will help increase your mathematical self-assurance.

Use All of Your Resources

Everyone has a different learning style, and there are plenty of resources out there to support all learners. When you get stuck on a math problem, think about the tools you have access to, and use them when applicable. Such resources may include flashcards, graphic organizers, study guides, interactive notebooks, and peer study groups. All of these are great tools to accommodate your individual learning style. Finding the tools and resources that work for your learning style will give you the confidence you need to succeed.

Realize That You Aren't Alone

Remind yourself that lots of other people struggle with math anxiety, including teachers, nurses, and even successful mathematicians. You aren't the only one who panics when faced with a new or challenging problem. It's probably much more common than you think. Realizing that you aren't alone in your experience can help put some distance between yourself and the emotions you feel about math. It also helps to normalize the anxiety and shift your perspective.

Ask Questions

If there's a concept you don't understand and you've tried everything you can, then it's okay to ask for help! You can always ask your teacher or professor for help. If you're not learning math in a traditional classroom, you may want to join a study group, work with a tutor, or talk to your friends. More often than not, you aren't the only one of your peers who needs clarity on a mathematical concept. Seeking understanding is a great way to increase self-confidence in math.

Remember That There's More Than One Way To Solve A Problem

Since everyone learns differently, it's best to focus on understanding a math problem with an approach that makes sense to you. If the way it's being taught is confusing to you, don't give up. Instead, work to understand the problem using a different technique. There's almost always more than one problem-solving method when it comes to math. Don't get stressed if one of them doesn't make sense to you. Instead, shift your focus to what does make sense. Chances are high that you know more than you think you do.

Visualization

Visualization is the process of creating images in your mind's eye. Picture yourself as a successful, confident mathematician. Think about how you would feel and how you would behave. What would your work area look like? How would you organize your belongings? The more you focus on something, the more likely you are to achieve it. Visualizing teaches your brain that you can achieve whatever it is that you want. Thinking about success in mathematics will lead to acting like a successful mathematician. This, in turn, leads to actual success.

Focus on the Easiest Problems First

To increase your confidence when working on a math test or assignment, try solving the easiest problems first. Doing so will remind you that you are successful in math and that you do have what it takes. This process will increase your belief in yourself, giving you the confidence you need to tackle more complex problems.

Find a Support Group

A study buddy, tutor, or peer group can go a long way in decreasing math-related anxiety. Such support systems offer lots of benefits, including a safe place to ask questions, additional practice with mathematical concepts, and an understanding of other problem-solving explanations that may work better for you. Equipping yourself with a support group is one of the fastest ways to eliminate math anxiety.

Reward Yourself for Working Hard

Recognize the amount of effort you're putting in to overcome your math anxiety. It's not an easy task, so you deserve acknowledgement. Surround yourself with people who will provide you with the positive reinforcement you deserve.

Remember, You Can Do This!

Conquering a fear of math can be challenging, but there are lots of strategies that can help you out. Your own beliefs about your mathematical capabilities can limit your potential. Working toward a growth mindset can have a tremendous impact on decreasing math-related anxiety and building confidence. By knowing the symptoms of math anxiety and recognizing common misconceptions about learning math, you can develop a plan to address your fear of math. Utilizing the strategies discussed can help you overcome this anxiety and build the confidence you need to succeed.

Thank You

We at Mometrix would like to extend our heartfelt thanks to you, our friend and patron, for allowing us to play a part in your journey. It is a privilege to serve people from all walks of life who are unified in their commitment to building the best future they can for themselves.

The preparation you devote to these important testing milestones may be the most valuable educational opportunity you have for making a real difference in your life. We encourage you to put your heart into it—that feeling of succeeding, overcoming, and yes, conquering will be well worth the hours you've invested.

We want to hear your story, your struggles and your successes, and if you see any opportunities for us to improve our materials so we can help others even more effectively in the future, please share that with us as well. **The team at Mometrix would be absolutely thrilled to hear from you!** So please, send us an email (support@mometrix.com) and let's stay in touch.

If you'd like some additional help, check out these other resources we offer for your exam:

http://MometrixFlashcards.com/MCA

Online Resources

Due to our efforts to try to keep this book to a manageable length, we've created a link that will give you access to all of your online resources:

mometrix.com/resources719/ssmcag8math

It's Your Moment, Let's Celebrate It!

Share your story @mometrixtestpreparation